Why Credit Can Be Greatly Expanded Without Adding to Inflation

By Lyndon H. LaRouche, Jr.

Why Credit Can Be Greatly Expanded Without Adding to Inflation

By Lyndon H. LaRouche, Jr.

EIR News Service • Washington, D.C.

On the cover: The world's largest high pressure reactor under construction in West Germany. (Photo: German Information Center.)

Contents

Editor's Note

This book is one of the best explications of Lyndon LaRouche's concept of a credit system--the least well understood aspect of any national growth strategy. It is not money which is the secret behind the rapid development of China and its growing network of development partners-- but credit!

Whether you are responsible for a nation's welfare, or that of a more modest portion of society, you will succeed if you master and participate in implementing the concepts in this book.

The text which follows is the original from 1980. In 1984, the international deliberations stimulated by Lyndon and Helga Zepp-LaRouche, led to the foundation of the Schiller Institute which became, along with the *Executive Intelligence Review* and much later, the LaRouche Political Action Committee, the primary vehicles for the rise of Mr. LaRouche's ideas to the extremely influential position they now hold globally in 2018. These ideas work. The predatory, monetarist, imperial ideas long promoted from London and Wall Street do not.

Author's Preface

During the recent several weeks, I have been traveling in Western Europe in a dual capacity, as spokesman for a current of the United States' Democratic Party, and as an economist dedicated to halting the present slide toward a probable 1981-1982 world depression. I have enjoyed the hospitality of a number of persons, including political, financial, and industrial personalities. Those persons typify, in total, a good portion of the policy outlook spectrum of Western continental Europe.

Although my principal obligation during these meetings has been to deliver information, I have been given much useful information in return. In particular, I have been aided in discovering what sort of information the widest assortment of business and political leaders currently require of me in published form.

This report, while intended to inform my friends and acquaintances among both major parties in the United States, is written with my friends and gracious hosts of France, Italy, India, Mexico, and the Federal Republic of Germany foremost in my mind's eye. The narrower object of this publication is to provide a summary of the answers which various of my friends and hosts have recommended I articulate in written form. The broader object of this report's circulation is to catalyze the establishment of new dimensions of transatlantic policy-formulating discussion, between the United States and our friends and allies of Western continental Europe.

1

As I shall elaborate the related point in the conclusion of this report, the very fact that this presently deepening crisis besieges our consciences with so many elements of justified deep anxiety is itself a symptom of the fact that we, collectively, have failed to think through the consequences of policies we have variously adopted or simply tolerated, over the span of, most emphatically, the greater part of the past 15 years.

Although Bilderberg and other policy-formulating institutions of transatlantic leading circles have proliferated during this period, the evidence at hand proves conclusively that some of the most decisive aspects of policy making have received variously inadequate or improperly formulated attention. Many of us have been, speaking collectively, caught unawares. This is chiefly because too many of such institutions as banking, industry, and trade unions have found leading scientists, bankers, and industrial executives—most emphatically—lacking the available personal time and available funding to conduct the kind of in-depth policy-formulating thinking and discussion which would have been needed to foresee the lawful emergence of the present crisis, and to formulate effective alternative policies.

Let us hope that it is not already too late to correct that serious omission. Let us hope that this report will prove itself an efficient contribution to the process of correcting that situation.

The specific, and most urgent, subject being treated in this report is the need to halt the present slide toward a world depression, through the early establishment of a new, gold-reserve-based monetary order. In response to the questions and challenges collectively emphasized during the indicated recent meetings, this report centers around summary treatments of three issues of policy pertaining to the establishment of a new, gold-reserve-based international rediscount institution as the keystone for the needed form of new monetary order.

The setting for this report is my considerably increased public authority as a leading economist. That condition is principally the outcome of the November 1979 publication of a computer-based forecast of the combined results for 1980 of both the October 1979 institution of the so-called Volcker measures in the United States and the leap in OPEC petroleum prices which occurred at the close of last year. The LaRouche-Riemann Model used to effect that November 1979 forecast has since proven empirically the only competent insight available into the underlying processes presently operating in world monetary and economic developments. This, the success of the LaRouche-Riemann Model, and the simultaneous relative discrediting of every other leading "econometric" forecast, has attached substantially increased public value to my analysis and policy recommendations among numerous persons from the world's best-informed circles.

The first among those three principal points to be summarized in this report is an outline of the basic steps for establishing *a new, gold-reserve-based international rediscount institution* on the cornerstone of what is

sometimes dubbed "Phase Two" of the existing European
Monetary System.   This action, while considered a
politically daring proposal by many, is only *politically*
daring.   Most qualified leading bankers and similarly
qualified persons readily agree that such a new institution
not only would work, in the technical sense of international
banking practices, but that it would provide a key
instrument for halting the present slide toward a new world
depression.

The objections and doubts arise as attention is shifted
from the technical provisions.   Objections appear as the
notion of the proposed new monetary order is situated
proximate to currently prevailing doctrines concerning
"reflation." Refutation of the objections arising in that way
leads this report to the second of the three featured points.

The second of those three featured points is the matter
of the mechanisms and results of *directed* channeling of the
kind of credit expansion proposed.

It is notable that this issue has arisen in the current U.S.
election campaign not only in connection with the pro-
European Monetary System policy of my own recent
campaign for the Democratic Party's presidential
nomination.

Considerable U.S. news media attention has been given
to independent candidate John B. Anderson's captious "it's
done with mirrors" attack on Governor Ronald Reagan's
proposal to effect tax reductions and increase military
spending simultaneously.   The wide acceptance of

Anderson's glibly incompetent opinion on this matter reflects the extent of wretchedness in economic thinking and education among a majority of U.S. influentials. Although Governor Reagan's specific tax-cut proposal is in fact unsound—as I reported in a nationwide half-hour television broadcast recently—the general thrust of Reagan's proposal is essentially correct, at least in contrast to the incompetent grounding of Representative Anderson's objections.

Treatment of the second of the three points here explains the essential reasons the objections to "reflationary" features of the proposed new monetary system are incompetent.

The discussion of the third of the three main points shifts the emphasis of our attention away from the mechanics of credit and monetary flows, to the proper basis for designing monetary policy: economic policy as such. It is in the domain of economics as such, apart from monetary theory, that the secrets of cyclical phenomena and inflation are unveiled. It is the ability to use credit to unleash a *potentially deflationary* high rate of capital investment in capital-intensive forms of agricultural, manufacturing, construction, mining, transportation, and energy production expansion, which uniquely justifies credit expansion.

It is in connection with this third point that the exceptional scientific authority of this reporter and his immediate collaborators is to be represented most emphatically.

Before turning to the three identified main points as such, two general sets of additional prefatory remarks are required. These two prefatory points included in this report are (1) summary identification of this reporter's unique scientific qualifications as an economist, and (2) outline of the way in which debate over current strategic crises and over credit and economic policies are presently juxtaposed in most leading circles of the transatlantic community. The second of the two introductory topics identifies the policy-making setting within which any present practical deliberations over monetary and economic policy must be situated at this juncture.

September 18, 1980

Lyndon H. LaRouche, Jr. is presently Chairman of the Advisory Committee for the National Democratic Policy Committee (U.S.A.), and was formerly one of the three candidates for the full course of the campaign for the Democratic Party's 1980 presidential nomination. He is otherwise known in circles of many industrialized and developing nations as a leading economist and policy-maker. He is also the husband of the European Labor Party's current President, Helga Zepp-LaRouche.

1

The Probable 1981-1982 Depression

The incontestable fact of the matter is this. If we leave out of account, for a moment, the expectation of continued rapid escalation in petroleum prices, and also the possibilities for explosion of one of the several principal strategic "hot spots" in the world today, it is feasible to forecast the general outlines of 1981-1982 economic developments in terms of presently prevailing trends in the policies of OECD nations. Such a forecast provides the indispensable statement of first approximation, which becomes, in turn, the setting of reference for weighing the effects of the critical, added developments temporarily left out of account in composing the initial forecast.

Those stipulations noted, the fact is that under continued support for the present policy trends of the International Monetary Fund, World Bank, and Basel Bank for International Settlements, *the United States economy is presently sliding into a new depression, and that slide is dragging most of the world into that same new general economic depression.*

The authority for such a firm judgment is as follows.

Throughout the 1970s to the present date, the principal movements in the United States' economy have correlated uniquely with the analysis provided by a computer-based analysis and forecasting method known as the LaRouche-

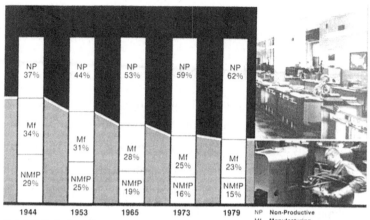

**Total U.S. Labor Force
by Percentage of Employment**

NP   Non-Productive
Mf   Manufacturing
NMfP   Non-Manufacturing Productive

The core problem underlying decay of the U.S. economy—a catastrophic decline in ratios of the American workforce employed productively vs. wasteful "service economy" bureaucratic employment.

Riemann Model. Economics Editor David Goldman has reviewed the conclusive evidence supporting that statement in the Sept. 2, 1980 issue of the weekly *Executive Intelligence Review.*[1]

As Goldman makes the point in that issue, all of the "competing" well-known econometric models, including those of the Federal Reserve System and Wharton Institute, have been proven totally incompetent by the devastating empirical evidence of the 1980 period to date. This has been stated publicly by U.S. Treasury Secretary G. William Miller.[2] The only forecast from any institution which has corresponded with the reality of post-October 1979 developments is the LaRouche-Riemann Model forecast first published in the *Executive Intelligence Review* issue of Nov. 6, 1979, and later elaborated in the January 1980 issue of the major-circulation scientific monthly, *Fusion* magazine.

To restate the point: *the LaRouche-Riemann Model is the only competent method for economic analysis and forecasting tool in existence at this time.*

Since the discredited econometric institutions have constructed their computer models according to specific brands of political-economic dogmas, it is implied—as is the case in fact—that it is the majority of prevailing brands of political-economic dogmas, including what is today still unfortunately accepted usually as "economics" in universities and among most professionals, which have suffered a sweeping refutation through the demonstrated incompetence of the econometric institutions basing their computer designs upon such dogmas.

The failures of the econometric institutions are, indeed, intrinsic to the dogmas behind the computer applications designs. One may say that the quality of this intrinsic failure is "axiomatic."

Two intrinsic, "axiomatic" incompetencies are common to all the popularized dogmas involved. First, any system of economic analysis which treats Gross Domestic Product (GDP, GNP), as presently defined in OECD countries' national income accounting procedures, as a correlative of economic growth is an intrinsically incompetent system of economic analysis. Second, any method of economic analysis and forecasting constructed on the basis of systems of linear equations for input-output relationships, is also intrinsically out of correspondence with the realities of economic processes—realities which are intrinsically "non-linear."

This does not mean that one entirely ignores GDP data. One has no choice today but to employ such data. The point is to recognize that total GDP includes two distinct subtotals, one of which reflects real economic output, whereas the complementary subtotal does not.

The first of these two subtotals, the portion which does correlate directly with real economic output, is the sum of the useful, tangible output of agriculture, manufacturing, construction, mining, energy production, and transportation of freight. *Useful* signifies that the model form of consumption of the product is as capital for production of tangible product or tangible consumer goods. These are useful because the process of consumption *regenerates* new, preferably enlarged and more productive, productive forces (productive labor and productive capacities) for the new cycle of production of useful, tangible product.

The notions of "useful" and "tangible" product output are conveniently combined into a single term, "productive output," or "regenerative" output.

The second category of GDP subtotal is a composite of administrative, service, military and wasteful activities. ("Military" is nonproductive, because *it is not economically regenerative* in mode of use.) Comparing whole economies to single industrial firms, the elements of this second category of subtotal represent "overhead burden."

Elements of this second category may be necessary, although they must not be misclassified as "productive" or as "real output," merely because they are proven to be necessary. Administration—the organization of government and of the processes of production and distribution—is categorically necessary. Services such as medicine and education are indispensable to maintaining the potential productivity of the labor force (in particular). Services such as science and engineering are indispensable to the maintenance and development of the productive process. Nonetheless, insofar as these necessary elements of administration and service enter into the determination of productivity, the benefits accrued in that way are fully embodied, as results, as final output, in the scale and productivity of the output of useful, tangible product.

Therefore, the act of adding the computed "value added" of administration, services, and military production to the "value added" of useful, tangible output, means to add the net contribution of administration and services *twice* to the total to calculate GDP!

For purposes of classroom and analogous pedagogy, it is useful to construct economic fantasies in which an entire economy, such as that of the Federal Republic of Germany, ceases all output of useful, tangible product, but employs the entire labor force in administrative, services, and military occupations. By setting the wage compensations for these nonproductive occupations ever higher, continuous growth of nominal GDP could be effected—with aid of spiraling indebtedness. Indeed, such fantasy scenarios merely illustrate in extreme terms the sorts of nonsensical trends in OECD economies which have been fostered under the influence of GDP-worshiping political-economic dogmas.

If nothing more than such hygienic correction of analytical procedures were introduced into present modes of governmental and other economic policy-relevant studies, a large step would be made toward making visible the true magnitude and horror of the past 15 years' accelerating slide toward the brink of a new conjunctural catastrophe.

To state competently the reasons "linear" economic models are fallacious in the simplest possible terms, the following summary is adequate at this stage of our report.

Since every state-of-the-art level of productive technology defines a certain set of conditions as "relatively finite natural resources," *an economy in a state approximating "zero technological growth" is an economy committing ecological suicide.* The mere continuation of existence of a nation at a net constant level of output, per capita consumption, and population density, requires a definable minimum rate of technological progress in the productive process. Below that rate of realized technological progress, the economy is dying; above that rate, the economy is becoming stronger, able to produce an increased standard of living even with increased population density.

Desirable shifts, upward, in realized technology improve, in first effect, the coefficients (effective productive social costs) for a previously defined range of "relatively finite natural resources." More significant degrees of cumulative technological progress cause a redefining of the domain of "relatively finite natural resources." Thus, today, the next two decades will witness global genocide in the order of billions of the world's population, unless nuclear energy production is aggressively proliferated. Furthermore, without reaching second-generation levels of leap in energy flux densities for fusion energy processes, mankind faces a second potential global, genocidal catastrophe during the course of the next century. Only if we effect commercial fusion energy production before the end of the present century will we later reach the still-higher level of new, fusion-based technologies, through which to break the limits of "relatively finite natural resources" as that domain is presently defined.

For such reasons, the notion of a "steady state" or "equilibrium model" economy is axiomatic professional incompetence, and is a murderous folly if incorporated into the policy making of nations.

A real economy must be defined as the outcome of ongoing strife between *developmental* (realized technological progress) and *devolutionary* impulses. Transformation of an economy in the direction of either impulse causes changes in not only the coefficients of input-output pathways, but structural changes in the characteristic pathways and constituent cell structure of the input-output matrix as a whole. In Mongeian words, the formerly characteristic "cross ratios" of the input-output manifold are superseded by new values.

In consequence of such considerations, econometric models congruent with the "systems philosophy" of Cambridge University's King's College—such as the Keynesian system, or the Viennese-positivist Mont Pelerin Society vulgarization of Keynes' system, might appear, falsely, to correlate with empirical economic reality under special conditions, over relatively short periods of persistence of such conditions. These must be periods of relative stability, during which the structural consequences of developmental or devolutionary trends appear to exert only marginal influence on total figures for such relatively smaller durations.

The moment the consequences of either major developmental or devolutionary tendencies begin to dominate the manifest economic results, the econometric approach to analysis and forecasting produces almost meaningless results—in more or less the fashion Treasury Secretary Miller observed the recent performance of the econometricians.

In physics terms, at such points the economy appears to have undergone a relative phase change, analogous to the changes of state which distinguish ice from water and both from steam.

Under such conditions, the process of successive transformations in economies must be studied as "non-linear" processes, as viewed from the standpoint of Bernhard Riemann's comprehension of the significance of Abelian functions of a higher order, just as such varieties of mathematical physics are presently indispensable for mastering "non-linear" phenomena, such as "solitons" in plasma physics.[3]

This does not imply that economies do in fact shift from a "linear" to "non-linear" state. The economic process is "non-linear" in all its phases. It is merely the case that the "non-linearity" of economic processes can be "smoothed over" by linear approximations under special conditions of constancy of apparent state during relatively shorter terms. Under circumstances of crisis, or any other sort of rapid structural transformations, it is the changes in characteristics corresponding to "non-linearity" which dominate, increasingly, even the shorter-term phenomena.

Hence, the incompetence of "linear models" is not merely a misfortune which comes into original existence at the point of crises; it is a continuous reality which comes violently to the surface under conditions of crisis.

The Author's Special Credentials

Although reference to this reporter's reputation as a leading economist has recently appeared in the major news media of some few nations, the quality and specifications of his detailed credentials are presently known but to a few outside of privileged insider circles. A brief summary of the matter is wanted here, for the information of a broader readership.

The author's special qualifications as an economist originate in a scientific breakthrough begun approximately 1952. The LaRouche-Riemann Model as presently elaborated is a direct, if much-delayed consequence of that 1952 discovery.

The reader will forgive us for continuing with resort to technical language again on this matter; the obligation to provide rigorous identification of some crucial points makes such technical-language intrusions necessary at this point of the report.

The relevant discovery was shaped in the following way. Through study of Georg Cantor's elaboration of the transfinite, this reporter was impelled to reject the generally adopted textbook and Einstein-Weyl notions of a Riemannian physical geometry, and to judge Riemann's actual outlook and work to be thoroughly coherent with Riemann's well-known, and much-libeled, habilitation dissertation on geometric hypotheses.

This discovery led to the author's crucial scientific breakthrough in economics. The methodological issue, more often situated for discussion in a physics context, as such, is crucial to understanding the basis for the unique success of the LaRouche-Riemann Model.

The issue is whether the physical universe can, or cannot be represented "in the very small" by tiny "tiles," each equatable to the classical Pythagorean method of measurement.

Gottfried Wilhelm Leibniz, in his attack on René Descartes concerning momentum, *implicitly* established systematic relativistic physics, denying there and elsewhere that the physical universe could be reduced in the small (the "infinitesimal" of his "delta") to anything methodologically analogous to what is often termed "Gaussian" methods of Pythagorean tiling.

This standpoint was revived under the leadership of the Leibnizian scientists Gaspard Monge and Lazare Carnot in France. This was reflected in the economics of Chaptal and Dupin, as well as the crucial work on the theory of functions by Fourier and Legendre. This viewpoint—of Leibniz, et al.—was reflected most strongly in the revolutionary progress of Germany's 19th century physics by the work of Karl Weierstrass, in one aspect, and by Riemann's advancement over the previous work of, explicitly, Abel and Legendre. Notably, in connection with the fundamental standpoint of Riemannian physics, expressed uniquely in his habilitation dissertation, Riemann credits the influence of Legendre.

Georg Cantor was the heir of Weierstrass, properly viewed, and is significant as a major contributor to elaborating the broader implications of Riemannian physics. Cantor inherited also Riemann's and Weierstrass's principal adversaries, notably the leading mid-19th century activist against the Leibnizian methodological tradition in German physics, Kronecker.

The division in continental-European scientific method, from the mid-19th century onward, was between the Leibnizian current on the one side (Monge, the Carnots, Fourier, Legendre, Weierstrass, Riemann, Cantor) and the eclectic, Anglo-Cartesian faction, exemplified by the "delphic" Cauchy in France, and by figures including Kronecker and Helmholtz in Germany. The crucial point of that opposition was—and continues to be—the issue of the nature of the physical geometry of the universe in the "very small."

Exemplary is Helmholtz's incompetent, but unfortunately influential attack on the essence of J. S. Bach, and of the German classical music system which Bach essentially established. There is no conceivable excuse for an educated physicist such as Helmholtz not to have known the geometric projection which precisely determines the value of tones in a well-tempered system, whose proof had been known since before the 10th-century A.D. al-Farrabi, and known in fact to the contemporaries of Plato.

Moreover, it has been demonstrated that a properly educated, preadolescent child can master adequately the geometric proof: that the principle of development of a musical composition, in terms of a domain of 24 combined major and minor keys, demands that tones be ordered according to the precisely determined values of the well-tempered system, and no other. What inorganic substances, such as vibrating strings and whistles, might prefer by way of a "more natural" tonal ordering, is of no interest to any human being, unless that person is, musically speaking, a vegetable.

We cite the example of Helmholtz's influential incompetence on the subject of tones here because his blunder respecting music is methodologically and conceptually analogous to the problems confronted by the rather commonplace academic's effort to linearize economic processes.

Methodologically, the problems of conceptualizing a well-tempered musical system and a real economy demand the identical outlook on the fundamental principles of physical science. Helmholtz's attempt to linearize the fundamentals of music is consistent with his sometimes "delphic" efforts to remove the active component of Riemannian physics by means of what is equivalent to a "Gaussian tiling" sort of linearization of physical geometry "in the very small." The notion of correcting such a misinterpretation of Riemann's physics points directly toward a solution to the most fundamental problem of economic analysis.

That is a fair description of the kinds of thinking processes which lead to replicating this reporter's scientific breakthrough in economics, begun in 1952.

Once we acknowledge the fact that economic processes are the end result of continuing contention between technological-developmental and technological-stagnation-devolutionary (entropic) impulses, it is immediately suggested by that discovery that the governing parameter for economic growth must be nothing other than a well-defined notion of a rate of technological progress. The problem encountered immediately at that point of insight is: how do we define "technology" as a parameter of a physical system?

Historically—that is, by ranking different modes of agricultural and industrial production according to the population-density potentials associated with such modes—the first-approximation parameter for economic development and growth is an increase in the per capita energy throughput of societies. For reasons we need not elaborate at this moment, we must supplement the notion of increased per capita energy throughput with the notion of rising energy-flux density of the sources of energy used. Similarly, it is the ratio of effective energy to total energy throughput ("free energy" ratio) which binds all of the notions of energy involved into a single, coherent conception.

We must therefore define "energy," in respect to economies being developed, as *energy input being self-organized into a higher state of quality of energy input.* Through the mediation of human creative advances in mastering the lawful ordering of the universe, the energy throughput of economies is transformed into ever higher equivalents of energy-flux density and free-energy ratios. *This image of self-transformation of an energetic process is usefully titled "negentropy."*

Broadly speaking, the ability of the human species to escape from a narrow set of "relatively finite natural resources" is a function of advances in the average energy-flux density of the energy sources used for production. In terms of approximation, the higher the energy-flux density of energy sources used for production, the greater the potential free-energy ratio, and the less the entropy loss.

The problem of accounting for the connection between rates of technological progress and economic growth must begin by restating the performance of economies in appropriate thermodynamic terms of reference, in terms of "negentropic rates" of thermodynamic transformation of the economy.

For those who recall the faddish ferment of the 1940s and early 1950s, it will not be surprising to learn that the writer's approach to this problem of economics, back in 1952 and afterwards, was situated in an environment saturated with the celebrity of Norbert Weiner's and others' casting of a doctrine of "information theory," and associated effluents. These included "linear programming" of the wartime Anglo-American "operations research" mobilization. It was this writer's hostility to reductionist notions of "information," including that embedded in Wiener's *Cybernetics*, which impelled this writer into the intense studies leading into the 1952 breakthrough. The same problem of reductionist linearization of mathematical economics was the writer's persisting adversary throughout his professional career as a management consultant, during the 1950s and beyond.

The polemical focus against "information theory" proved to be—and is—a useful setting for uncovering the required notion of "rates of technology," provided one properly situates the fundamental fallacy of "information theory" methodologically. It is the methodological issue which separates Riemann from his adversary and plagiarist, J. C. Maxwell, Kronecker from Weierstrass and Cantor, and Helmholtz from a competent conception of tonality. It is the methodological issue of counterproductive attempts to linearize the physical geometry of the universe "in the very small." The standpoint of Riemannian physical geometry, as defined in coherence with his habilitation dissertation (not the "Gaussian tiling" misrepresentation of his geometric physics), provides the critical basis for overcoming the reductionist fallacies of "information theory."

We properly define the consequences of realized scientific discovery by measuring economic processes as Riemannian *thermohydrodynamic* phase-space processes, *according to the conception of a Riemannian multiply-connected manifold required by the habilitation dissertation.* The causal element of technological progress is the distinctive perfectability of the human mind, the power to discover, communicate, and apply qualitative breakthroughs in the comprehension of the lawful ordering of the universe, as *itself a congruent, special kind of multiply-connected manifold.* Thus, we properly measure scientific progress in terms of the actual and implied consequences of such progress, in the resulting reorganization of the productive process. This result is to be measured in *negentropy* of the socially-thermodynamically defined social-productive process as a whole.

That sort of discovery, the breakthrough accomplished by the writer back in 1952, has two implied directions of outcome. *On the one side*, concentrating on the determining relations reflected "in the very small," it leads toward a convergence of economic science and a generalized, Riemann-derived thermohydrodynamics. *On the other side*, those rigorous, more sophisticated considerations guide one to determine what less technically sophisticated form of analysis of economic processes, as economic processes' accounting terms are more commonly defined, is the correct choice for national income accounting and related practices.

The writer's continuing work in the first direction surfaced publicly chiefly in a few references up into the mid-1960s. It was during the course of the 1970s that the writer's initial insights of 1952 began to be publicly elaborated in detail in conjunction with cross-fertilization by treatment of leading problems of contemporary plasma physics research.

Emphasizing the application of the second direction first, that background governed the writer's approach to economic analysis and forecasting, in the more conventional sense of such practice, leading to a successful pre-analysis of the causes, duration, and character of the 1957-1958 U.S. recession by early 1957. Encouraged by that initial success, beginning early 1958 and continuing into late 1959, the writer was emboldened to project the

general outlines of an emerging breakdown of the Bretton
Woods system.

The main points of that 1958-1959 forecast are relevant
information for the present, since this information defines
what could and should have been more generally foreseen
as far back as 1960. The fact that so definite a process of
devolution of the Bretton Woods system was looming,
without manifestly competent recognition of that fact in
leading policy-making circles, defines the goad which has
spurred the writer's continuing efforts into special
directions, including various unavoidable detours, over the
course of the past two decades.

During the course of the 1958-1959 studies the writer
determined and reported that:

(1) Because of the developmental impulse centered in
the capital development of Western continental Europe and
Japan, the threatened breakdown of the Bretton Woods
system would be postponed until the middle of the 1960s,
after which a succession of general monetary crises would
bring the economies of such a decaying monetary system
into a depression collapse far worse than that experienced
between the two preceding World Wars of this century—
under the "Versailles system."

(2) On the basis of the manifest dominant beliefs and
habituated impulses of ruling institutions, the succession of
worsening monetary crises would prompt influential
financier agencies, analogous to the 1930s London "short-
term credit" committee, to opt for a new form of fascistic

austerity order, as the London committee had forced Adolf Hitler on Germany in 1932-1933.

(3) There existed no possibility for avoiding this pattern through any reform *within the axiomatic terms of the Bretton Woods system*. Only a comprehensive monetary reform, free of the intrinsic fallacies of the Bretton Woods system, would halt the process of economic devolution toward barbaric conditions.

The beginning of the writer's emergence into national and international notability began with the crisis of 1971. The fact that the writer had been warning vigorously of the imminence of just such a crisis over the period following the 1967-1968 sterling-dollar crisis, greatly increased the number and aggregate institutional influence of the writer's collaborators. In the immediate aftermath of the August 1971 crisis, the writer initiated the establishment of a special institution to monitor the combined monetary, economic, and political correlatives of the deepening crisis —independent of the resources otherwise represented by largely disinformational news media and incompetently advised financial and business publications.

That institution became in 1974 the international political-intelligence news service, NSIPS, whose regular publications include the weekly *Executive Intelligence Review*. During the same year, the writer, his collaborators, and a number of leading plasma physicists jointly sponsored the establishment of a new scientific and educational institution, the Fusion Energy Foundation, a scientific association which now has more than 12,000 members in the United States and a circulation of its monthly magazine currently exceeding a quarter million copies. Although a number of the writer's immediate collaborators participating in contributing support to that latter institution's efforts were qualified scientists or engineers in their own right, the principal part of the contribution to support of the work of the FEF from the writer and his collaborators has been emphasis on Riemannian physical geometry as the approach to plasma physics experimental hypothesis, and the developing of a leading competence in the economics of energy development.

These matured resources enabled the writer and his collaborators to introduce the appropriate physics to the computer-based application of his method of economic analysis and forecasting. Thus, the LaRouche-Riemann Model.

The 1981-1982 General Forecast

Since the LaRouche-Riemann Model is the only competent forecasting instrument for the conditions of this present period, there exists presently no competent basis for objection to the judgments of the LaRouche-Riemann Model.

First, even without resorting to the model, mere observance of our exposure of the fraud of GDP, given above, suffices to prove conclusively that the United States economy has been sliding into a new depression—or, at least, toward such an outcome—since the October 1979 initiation of the "Volcker measures." Similarly, taking into account the impossibility of reversing the present "Third World debt crisis" pattern under continued hegemony of the presently constituted IMF, World Bank, and Basel BIS, plus acknowledgement of the effects of continued rise in petroleum prices, shows that the combined, self-imposed "controlled disintegration" of the British, Canadian, and U.S. economies is already pushing the relatively healthier economies of Western Europe and of Japan toward participation in a general new depression.

The use of the LaRouche-Riemann Model computer analysis enables us to refine our initial, broad assessment.

It should be interpolated here that the computer application, which was initiated in December 1978, has been improved in two directions, successively, since the initial run reported during early 1979. The data base has been expanded and refined continuously, to the point that the model now takes the U.S. economy together with the non-China developing nations sector and Western Europe. Simultaneously, improved mathematical procedures and associated improved programming algorithms have been introduced. The data base is the responsibility of *EIR* Economics Editor David Goldman and his associates; the computer modeling is the responsibility of a plasma physicist, Dr. Steven Bardwell, and Dr. Uwe Parpart. The concepts and procedures used have all been adopted in consultation with this reporter. The most recent computer run, completed during mid-September, includes the data base for Western Europe and the developing nations sector.

The forecasts reflected in this report arc based on that most recent run.[4]

Barring new, exogenous interventions, such as new petroleum crises, the present policy pattern of OECD nations plus the IMF, World Bank, and BIS ensures that the present pattern of depression slide will continue into some point in 1981. Under present trends, at that point in 1981, the depression will appear to many credulous persons to have "bottomed out." The probability of such an inflection is enhanced on condition that wage-rate structures and governmental, social, and other services are significantly savaged by the effects of the depression slide to promise temporary recovery in profit-rates.

Contrary to credulous observers of that future interval, that sort of apparent, temporary "bottoming out" of the depression is but a lull, preceding the unleashing of the major and steepest part of the descent: a mere interval of inflection preceding the main force of the storms of economic collapse.

It should be emphasized that the Carter administration and various other, presumably authoritative voices in the United States are simply lying outright whenever they report that the worst of the 1980 "recession" is over. In part, that official and semi-official lying is an echo of the current election campaign period.

However, there are darker aspects to this lying than the mere practice of fraudulent campaign propaganda. The Carter "reindustrialization" package for the United States, integral to the proposal to make it essentially a major coal-exporting nation, is explicitly dedicated to wiping out a major portion of whole categories of basic industry in the United States. Old Hjalmar Schacht would blush in horror at the savagery of the forced depression collapse the Carter administration plans for the United States as soon as the 1980 general election is ended.

So, in addition to the savagery of depression collapse for the 1981-1982 period already built into existing IMF, BIS, and Carter administration monetary and energy policies, that administration plans to add willful, dirigist destruction of whole categories of basic industries, plus hideous triaging of other categories.

Apart from the forecasts provided by the LaRouche-Riemann Model, the general direction which the 1981 world economy is moving is already widely known among leading business circles as well as policy-making think tanks directing international financial institutions and governments. One might imagine that industry circles of the United States and Europe would object strenuously to continuing such devolutionary policies. Correspondingly, one might imagine that general monetary reform, based on the cornerstone of "Phase Two" of the European Monetary System, might be a proposal which would be energetically pushed forward by industry, with most energetic support from trade union and farmer organizations.

No such broad-based opposition to a continuing depression slide is manifest. Why not? It is implicit in such evidence, as is the case in fact, that a large section of financial and industrial management has been more or less saturated with advice to the effect that such a hideous depression is even desirable at this time.

At this point, we focus attention on the most commonplace arguments advanced in favor of such a depression. In the next of the two prefatory sections of this report, we focus more narrowly on the way in which the presently worsening strategic crisis bears on the issues of depression and monetary reform.

What admirers of Britain's Thatcher government see as a hygienic purging of accumulated industrial rubbish and fat, is in fact a process of destroying large portions of the basic structure of productive potential of affected nations. We may, in fairness, concede that much of the structure has been reduced to marginality by accumulated obsolescence. Much of the structure of basic industry and agriculture is already ruined, by combined effects of obsolescence and spiraling debt burdens. It is argued by some of Thatcher's admirers that purging such diseased elements, plus massive cuts in wage and social service structures, is a desirable—if *regrettably* desirable—action, on which to found the rudiments of a successful economic recovery.

There are two obvious, gross fallacies in such argumentation in favor of Thatcher-style "controlled disintegration."

First, as Middle East experience with the Mongol invasion illustrates, *inviting Genghis Khan to turn one's culture into rubble, and the surviving remnant of one's populations to a superstitious, drug-ridden rabble, has never demonstrated empirically its merits as an economic recovery measure.*

Second, destroying indebted entities without canceling the indebtedness of those entities, has the effect of multiplying the inflationary impulse which is essentially embedded in an excessively high ratio of current debt service obligations to the allocable margins of current income.

Granted, Hjalmar Schacht appears—to some—to have verged upon success with his Rentenmark, Mefo Bill, and his various, associated, often savage austerity measures of the Weimar and early Third Reich periods. Jacques Rueff's published study of Schacht's methods proves conclusively that an estimate of Schacht's near success is intrinsically incompetent.[5] The fact that Schacht opposed certain later developments in Third Reich policy cannot be construed to suggest that it was anything but the outcome of Schacht's measures which impelled the Reich to occupy and loot successively Austria, Czechoslovakia, Poland, the Low Countries, France, and most of Europe, in order to minimize the self-cannibalization of German industry, agriculture, and labor force intrinsic to Schacht's measures.

Jacques Rueff's apt characterization of Schachtian methods, as emphasized by Rueff in a meeting with this reporter back in 1976, was "inflation turned inward against the economic base." A comparison of Rueff's published analysis of this phenomenon with the published studies by this reporter and his associates, is the exemplary truth, to be contrasted with the mythologies of British intelligence's postwar Wilton Park "brainwashing" exercise.

The shocking fact is that the same sort of policy is being repeated, on a much larger scale today. Chiefly as a consequence of the popularized frauds of Wilton Park, et al., the crucial lessons of Schacht's Weimar and Third Reich experiments are either virtually unknown, or are simply ignored by most OECD policy-influentials today. Then, as now, there were two, complementary features to the emergence and evolution of the Third Reich.

There was then, as now, the exotic ideological side. Then, it was the origins of the inner circle of the Nazi gang from British-sponsored cults of Vienna and the Wittelsbach's Haushofer-pivoted intelligence community. Today, it is the mixture of Blavatskyian counter-cultural ideology with the neo-Malthusianism of the Club of Rome: billions of "excess eaters" are to be eliminated from the world's population, chiefly by "regrettably necessary" famine and epidemic. The year 2000 is most often cited by Club of Rome, British, and U.S.A. sponsors of *that greatest genocide in all human history!*[6]

This exotic, ideological aspect was then, as now, complemented by the spiral of austerity, then focused most sharply on Versailles-looted Weimar Germany. Then, as now, the lunatic ideological instrument, the Nazi cult then, like the Club of Rome-centered "environmentalist" neo-Malthusianism of today, was brought into political power to implement a further degree of austerity which had become impossible under any approximation of rationalist parliamentary government.

From the inside of early 1930s Germany, it tends to be the case that the choice of Hitler appears to be explained fully by the decisions of certain German influentials. That considered view of the matter is the fallacy of composition used to construct the predominantly fraudulent Wilton Park mythology. From the outside of 1930s Germany, the decision to put Hitler into power—and to remove Schleicher—was conduited through the London short-term credit committee. By adapting, "realistically," "pragmatically," to the path of choices openly preferred by leading London circles of that time, as well as 1932-33 editions of the *New York Times*' front-page news features and editorials, the German influentials involved found themselves "of their own free will" preferring the sorts of alternatives Hitler dictated to Germany, in fact, by way of circumstances dictated by London.

Naturally, in the immediate aftermath of war, the British intelligence services concocted the varieties of "collective guilt" mythologies which diverted attention away from London's leading role in imposing Hitler upon Weimar Germany. In consequence of the imposition of that fraudulent Wilton Park thesis upon the textbooks and news media myth-making of the OECD and other nations, the crucial lessons of the Schacht experiment are variously unknown or diplomatically ignored today.

So, the proposals of such neo-Schachtians as Friedrich von Hayek, Milton Friedman, and Paul A. Volcker confront us today: in such forms as the policies of the Thatcher and Carter governments, in the form of IMF "conditionalities," in the form of World Bank "conditionalities," in the murderous austerity endorsed by the Basel Bank for International Settlements, and, of course, the ideologues of the Club of Rome and the neo-Blavatskyians of the present.

From the vantage point of political economy, the moral devolution of the Third Reich represents essentially the succession of moral changes in state accompanying and energized by a willful acceptance of policies of monetarist-impelled economic devolution. Today, even persons who are doubtless horrified by the memory of Nazism propose policies practically consistent with Club of Rome-pivoted proposals to reduce the world's population by billions by approximately the year 2000.

A policy of devolution (austerity of the Thatcher and Carter government forms) means an inevitable classification of increasing portions of the world's population as "unwanted eaters." *Economic devolution means reducing the population-density potential.* The political problem intrinsic to a policy of reducing willfully population density potential is what choice of means shall be adopted for eliminating the "excess population."

Schacht's experiment was a hideous failure. The resurrections of such austerity policies, on a larger scale, today, probably means *the end of a civilization which has become morally unfit to survive.* Clearly, since many of the influentials trapped into admiration of Mrs. Thatcher's neo-Schachtianism are otherwise honorable, moral, and intelligent persons, the problem which confronts us on this account is their failure to think through a policy to its intrinsic consequences.

Looking at this matter from the other side of its implications, we focus on the fact that most of the admirers of the Thatcher model are sincerely and justly concerned to purge the poisonous consequences of the venereal-like "British disease" from the OECD economies. Having failed to think the problem through adequately, they see only the purging of obsolescence and the reversal of institutionalized social policies which have increased the overhead costs of societies while shifting the labor force away from emphasis on production of useful, tangible output. Viewing the Thatcher model too narrowly, they see, one-sidedly, only the purging of decay, and not the principal more general consequences.

To this aspect of the expressed sympathy for the Thatcher model, we are obliged to present the alternative policy which effects the desired result, without the Schachtian devolutionary "side effects."

Exemplary is the problematic case of the United States. At the beginning of postwar conversion from military production, the proportion of the total U.S. labor force employed in producing useful, tangible wealth was between 62 percent and 63 percent. Over the period 1946-1955, this percentile did not fall below 55 percent. In 1979, leaving out of account the fact that about 6 percent of the U.S. labor force has been dropped from official statistics for cosmetic reasons, the percentile was 38 percent, and falling rapidly.[7]

It is the post-1958 U.S. policy, of shifting the United States from its past character as an industrial society, toward becoming a "services-oriented society," which accounts for the plunge in the percentile of the labor force employed productively as operatives in combined agriculture, manufacturing, construction, energy production, mining, and transportation. This problem is compounded by growing obsolescence and decay in the productive capital of most categories of manufacturing and mining. The collapse of U.S. productivity, resulting from such a "services-oriented" policy, has been compounded by the manufacturing of variously nonproductive or marginally productive make-work employment, chiefly in monstrously inefficient forms of labor-intensive unskilled and semiskilled services employment.

The aggravating feature of this problem is the continued use of the fraudulent "Total GNP'" statistic as if it were a competent measure of national output.

The services-oriented policy has shifted the national cost of output from a predominantly productive cost emphasis of over 62 percent in 1946 to less than 38 percent in 1979, thus increasing the overhead burden, while reducing the economic basis for carrying that overhead burden. In consequence of a shift away from long-term credit and investment for productive capital formation—except, after 1967, into "technetronic" categories[8]—the productivity of the shrinking productive sector of the U.S. economy has eroded. Following 1972-74, the emphasis on substituting labor-intensive employment for energy-intensive employment has caused the former erosion of industrial productivity to be superseded by a spiraling absolute decline in productivity.

In this circumstance, if we permit the United States to proceed with the Carter administration's recently proposed "reindustrialization" package, whole categories of basic industry will be eliminated, while large sections of other categories will be "triaged." This means a savage depletion of the already shrunken productive base, and a savage increase in the already cancerous ratio of overhead burden to productive basis. The U.S. economy's productive base will be so shrunken that the nation will lack the existing productive capacity even to maintain itself, to say nothing of launching the expansion in productive output needed to bring the economy above "break-even." True, some varieties of draconian measures are urgently required—but which?

We must have a savage reversal in credit policies, drying up flows of increased credit into every category but increases in the scale and productivity of operatives employed in agriculture, manufacturing, construction, mining, energy production and transportation. Obsolete capacity must be stripped of its residual capital by continued production which uses up that obsolete capacity, and transforms the capital so liquified into new financial capital for investment in modern replacement technologies. Credit policies must, in short, cause a war-mobilization variety of forced-draft utilization of all salvageable and better-than-salvageable production capacity for civilian output, with emphasis on modern capital goods production.

Wage rates for unskilled and semiskilled labor-intensive services employment must be kept marginally, but significantly, below those set for productive employment of operatives in agriculture, manufacturing, mining and so forth. Excepting for skilled administrators, scientists, engineers, physicians, teachers and such essential cadre-categories of professional services, unskilled or semiskilled administration and services employment must be pegged at significantly lower rates of increases in hourly compensation and fringe benefits than employment of semiskilled productive operatives. We must impel the majority of unskilled and semiskilled administrative and service workers to desire and seek out the more advantageous employment conditions of productive labor.

These measures must be complemented by drastic shifts in taxation policies. True depreciation levels must be defined (current replacement of current state-of-the-art equivalent to former state-of-the-art being depreciated), and must replace historical accounting methods for calculating depreciation in all affected OECD and developing nations. Tax exemptions for depreciation, amortization, depletion, and investment tax credits must be most generous, and such tax benefits must be extended to investors and bank depositors as well as the firm or farm making the capital investment. A high rate of progressive income tax should be imposed upon all categories of income which are not sheltered under such favorable tax treatment of productively invested household savings and profits.

Governments must act in concert to create stable, long-term, profitable markets for high-technology productive investment throughout the world.

By such means, emphasizing nuclear technologies as the most massive component and leading edge of the new investment boom, we must force the economies infected with various degrees of the "British disease" *to produce their way out of the present mess*, by shifting emphasis away from labor-intensive services, toward skilled employment in high-technology modes of basic production of useful, tangible wealth.

This requires, of course, a subsumed, ruthless determination to outlaw the vetoing of technological progress by the relatively tiny "environmentalist" minorities. The "environmentalists" are, essentially, a fringe minority group, which therefore has no democratic right to impose its eccentric dogmas on the majority. This minority's definition of its interests and rights is irrational in form and irrationalist in method. Hence, it has in fact no actual individual or minority group rights under rational law which are binding on society in respect to the urgent, opposing needs and rights of society as a whole. What can we say of a group which ignores the fact that, in contrast to the many deaths caused by riding of bicycles, not one nuclear-related death has been caused by the operation of a commercial reactor?

Furthermore, since delay or constriction of the proliferation of nuclear energy development means the assured death of hundreds of millions through famine and epidemic disease, *the "environmentalists" are implicitly, potentially the greatest mass murderers in human history to date.* No minority has the right to oblige a majority to murder itself, simply to reduce population densities to levels consistent with the potentials of the sort of barbaric neo-Malthusian utopias demanded by the contemporary rock-drug counterculture.

Notes

1. David Goldman, "Why the EIR Model Beat Wall Street's 1980 Predictions," *Executive Intelligence Review*, Sept. 2, 1980, pp. 16-20. Using the LaRouche-Riemann Econometric Model, the *EIR* on Nov. 6, 1979 projected that then-adopted Federal Reserve credit policies and oil price increases would cause a 15 percent drop in U.S. industrial production during the eight quarters of 1980-81, with most of the drop to occur in 1980. The projection has proven accurate both overall and sector by sector within the productive economy. Ostensibly prestigious forecasters like Data Resources, Inc., Wharton Econometric Associates, and Chase Econometrics, on the other hand, published projections in April 1980 whose production and inflation indices were six percentage

points or more off the mark for the ensuing second-quarter alone.

2. Miller declared in March 1980, "All econometrics have been wrong. I think we have to recognize that there isn't an econometric model of any type that has been able to predict what has happened.

3. The early 19th century Danish mathematician Abel developed the modern form of solution to Legendre's problem of finding the circumference of an ellipse. An Abelian function is the general form of the type of function that arises in attempting to determine the length of a curve which has variable curvature. The simplest is the elliptical function which arises in determining the circumference of an ellipse. Riemann saw how the analytic properties of Abelian functions were a powerful tool for solving differential equations that arise in physics.

4. "Austerity Leads to 'Double-Dip' 1981 Collapse," EIR, Sept. 2, 1980, 24.

5. For Rueff's treatment of Schacht's incompetence, sec his *The Age of Inflation* (Chicago: Regnery, 1964) and *The Monetary Sins of the West* (New York: Macmillan, 1972).

6. Since 1967, worldwide coordination of neo-Malthusian "Year 2000" ideological projects has been centered in the Science Policy Research Unit, a division of the British Tavistock Institute created for that purpose by the British Royal Institute for

International Affairs. In 1971 the Club of Rome commissioned Jay Forrester and Dennis Meadows, *The Limits to Growth: A Report for the Club of Rome Project on the Predicament of Mankind* (Cambridge: MIT Press, 1972); the latter project otherwise known as "Mankind 2000." In the U.S. the neo-Malthusian "2000" policy and ideology are institutionalized in the White House Commission on Environmental Quality, *Global 2000 Report to the President* (Washington, D.C., 1980); and New York Council on Foreign Relations, *1980s Project* (New York: McGraw-Hill, 24 vols., 1977-81).

7. Lyndon H. LaRouche, Jr., "Milton Friedman: The Man Behind Carter's Fascist Economics" (New York: Citizens for LaRouche, April 1980).

8. "Technetronic society" alludes most emphatically to a publication authored in 1967 by Zbigniew Brzezinski, *America in the Technetronic Age.* This paper appeared in the context of a study used to motivate the phasing down of NASA, as part of an overall deindustrialization of the United States. That proposal was conduited through British intelligence's Tavistock Institute. Britain's proposal to end U.S. emphasis on industrial progress included a report by Dr. Anatol Rapaport. a U.S. associate of the Tavistock Institute.

2

The Strategic Equation

The majority among influential strategists, financiers, industrialists, and so forth thus far encountered on both sides of the Atlantic during most recent months have stated that they agree either entirely or about 90 to 95 percent with this reporter's analysis of the strategic situation. The emphasis is to be placed on the term "analysis." Unfortunately, to date, fewer are prepared to accept fully this reporter's proposed remedies for that strategic problem.

For a period, extending from this past spring into the summer months, there was a widespread fear among policy influentials, especially in Western Europe, that continued economic devolution of the OECD nations would produce inevitably an accelerated relative growth in Soviet strategic advantage over the course of the 1980s. This fear was mixed with and dominated by a well-grounded perception that the proliferation of "hot spots" in Asia, Africa, and Latin America, would lead to the sort of strategic miscalculation resulting either in a general nuclear war or a strategically decisive backdown and humiliation of relatively inferior U.S.-led military forces.

In consequence of such fears, many among such influentials tended to oppose the "controlled disintegration" policies of the Carter administration. The typical outlook of this sort was twofold. First, without revival of the high-

"An accelerated relative growth in Soviet strategic advantage over the course of the 1980s" is threatened by continued economic devolution of the Western capitalist nations.

technology industrial growth of the OECD nations and their developing sector capital goods markets, it would be economically impossible to maintain either quantitative or qualitative rough parity with Warsaw Pact capabilities.

Second, IMF "conditionalities," "antinuclear proliferation," and related devolutionary policies imposed upon developing nations foster the economic and social preconditions for violent political instabilities within those nations and the regions they represent. Economic development will not effect political stability in such nations and regions by itself, but it is an indispensable sort of included precondition for reversing that deepening instability which promotes the proliferation and worsening of "hot spots."

In other words, even many who otherwise admired the "Thatcher model," were inclined to reject such a generalized Thatcher policy, *for strategic reasons.*

The principal counter-argument encountered was and continues to be essentially the following: "I agree with that analysis—up to a point. I insist that that analysis overlooks one major additional consideration. The Soviet Empire is about to be plunged into a raging internal crisis." From the mouth of Zbigniew Brzezinski, the argument was more extreme: We have the Soviet Empire tightly encircled, Brzezinski gloated manically during a recent briefing session. Now, his circles argue, we shall proceed to destabilize this tightly encircled domain from within.

The recent, preliminary, limited success of the Brzezinski-linked destabilization within Poland swung numerous waverers on both sides of the Atlantic around to full or conditional support of the strategic outlook reflected through Brzezinski.

The point is more or less as follows. If the Warsaw Pact is about to undergo accelerating internal destabilization, then future Soviet strategic development will be curtailed accordingly. That estimation fosters the assumption that, under conditions of deteriorating Soviet strategic potential, the OECD nations can safely bear that reduction of their own strategic potentials which is inherent in a Thatcher-model "controlled economic disintegration."

In such a setting, occupation with the strategic situation is restricted relatively to European efforts to prevent a nuclear strategic confrontation over the relatively short term. Alternatives to the Thatcher-model orientation, such as implementing "Phase Two" of the European Monetary System, tend to be opposed, or pushed onto the "back burner," simmering for want of sufficiently broad support.

I wish I could receive one deutschemark for each time since November 1917 a prominent figure has authoritatively predicted the looming internal collapse of the Soviet economy. Moreover, the mere fact that British intelligence and related entities have well-placed agents of influence in elements of the Soviet and Eastern European commands ignores the fact that similar conditions have existed since the Bolshevik seizure of power. The subsuming fallacy of all such wishful anticipation of imminent Soviet collapse, is the methodological error of extrapolating from isolated factors, failing to comprehend the way in which the Soviet process as a whole compensates for the influence of such factors.

To go directly to the most crucial point now, before exploring the Soviet economy's condition, the case in which the Soviet command sees itself being pushed to a point of no return in reduced strategic capabilities *is the point at which the Soviet command will willfully risk total war in order to break the geopolitical vise by whatever means the problem at hand prescribes as wanted for a decisive, successful solution. In other words, the assumption that Brzezinski and Company might be able to succeed in deploying internal destabilization of the Warsaw Pact to such indicated effects is itself the specific sort of strategic miscalculation which leads toward general nuclear war.*

The principle involved has been a repeatedly corroborated axiom of modern military science since Niccolo Machiavelli. A major power, confronted with a threatened annihilation of its *political integrity*, will deploy its fullest means of destruction required to destroy assuredly the agency responsible for this threat.

For related reasons, but for the December 1941 Pearl Harbor attack, it would have been nearly impossible to mobilize the United States for World War II at the pace and on the scale which did occur. Or, but for the destruction of General MacArthur's Philippine-based complement of the U.S. Army Air Force, shortly after Pearl Harbor, MacArthur would have been able to administer the greater penalties to the Japanese forces which would have altered the initial course of the war in the Pacific theater, thus altering the U.S. orientation, and moderating the tempo of war mobilization.

What sometimes appear to be the decisive, isolatable political-strategic factors in a situation prove, under "phase-space" changes in the strategic situation, to have been relatively mere ephemerals. The defeat of the French and allied forces in 1940 is exemplary of the consequences of strategic assumptions premised on the algebraic calculation of combinations of isolable factors.

Otherwise, Eastern Europe and the Soviet Union are by no means homogeneous.

With the UNNRA, Marshall Plan and other Churchill-directed measures in Eastern Europe during the immediate postwar period, Moscow's perception of the Anglo-American commitment to preparations for "preemptive war" at that time (e.g., Operation "Dropshot") impelled Moscow to consolidate Eastern Europe politically as a forward base for Soviet strategic deployment. Thus, the nations of Eastern Europe acquired improvised governments, created under the direction of Soviet bayonets, in accordance with perceived dictates of Soviet strategic interests. That heritage persists, although in considerably modified circumstances today.

These states were created largely by promoting from within the populations of the occupied Eastern European nations political personalities, factions, and social strata viewed by Moscow as relatively more agreeable to Soviet strategic interests for that region. The present socialist institutions of these states are not to be considered as predominantly artificial now on account of such "artificial" beginnings. Any set of institutions which function as instruments of organized national life, shape the habits and consciences of the populations integrated into those institutions. Nonetheless, noting the major differences in character among these states, they do not typify the character of the population and institutions of the Soviet Union itself.

Although the Soviet Union is fairly described as "socialist" in its principal institutions, it is a grave error to assume that the Soviet institutions are premised in any degree on an ideology of "a global communist conspiracy." The Soviet Union is a highly nationalistic state, which happens to premise the development and management of that state on nationalized ownership and direction of the principal means of production. That is to emphasize that the predominant, the essential underlying determinant of Soviet behavior is an extreme, war-, and cold-war hardened Soviet nationalism.

The fact that leading elements of the Soviet command accept Moscow versions of "orthodox Marxism-Leninism" as a mode for interpreting processes, does not mean that the underlying criteria in whose service Marxist-Leninist algorithms are deployed are themselves engendered from within a body of ideology describable as Marxism-Leninism. Under conditions of crisis, it is the Soviet nationalist impulse which governs, and which will, under such circumstances, extensively reshape Marxist-Leninist ideology in conformity with the dictates of nationalist impulses.

Some statesmen, news media and others have been recently so self-righteously self-deluded by official postures of denunciation of the Soviet operations in Afghanistan that those persons, and similarly wishfully self-misguided persons, overlook the crucial-experimental significance of Afghanistan for assessing the innermost criteria of Soviet policy responses today.

As I predicted a massive Soviet deployment into Afghanistan in the spring of 1979,[9] outlining the reasons such a development would uniquely confirm my strategic analysis, this development conclusively establishes a governing Soviet determination to draw the line ruthlessly against any further advances of the sort of geopolitical deployments variously propounded by Henry A. Kissinger and Zbigniew Brzezinski.

The effect of the Polish destabilization did not initiate, at least not predominantly, a rolling wave of further destabilizations of the East bloc. Predominantly, it provoked Moscow into a posture of towering rage, combined with a resolution to play out the Polish destabilization and similar manifestations by entirely different scenarios than London and Mr. Brzezinski intend to set into motion by such means.

The leading forces in Moscow today were in secondary levels of political and military command during the last war, with most hanging in their closets the uniforms to be adorned publicly should the tempo of confrontation appear to warrant such displays. The successor generation in the command structure is persons in their forties and fifties, who matured under conditions of the Cold War and the phase-change in Soviet long-term policy correlated with the 1962 Cuban missile crisis. Otherwise, the best capability of the Soviet command, relatively speaking, lies on the military side, not the political side. Under conditions of intensified geopolitical confrontation, the sort of thinking characteristic of the military command will spill over increasingly into the form of the political-strategic decisions of the political command as a whole.

The Soviet command is now preparing to fight, and if necessary, fight to win World War III. The towering rage evoked in leading Moscow circles by the recent Poland events has accelerated that process. This is manifest more clearly in the overtones of recent Soviet conduct than overt gestures. They are now seeking to retaliate with exploited opportunities for strategic surprise, assessing the weak flanks of the adversary's geopolitical position.

They will not sit in a defensive posture respecting destabilizations attempted in Eastern Europe. That posture would be military-strategic insanity, and therefore will not be the disposition of the Soviet command as a whole. They will deploy into what they perceive to be the Atlantic Alliance's geopolitical flanks, to compensate for the marginal weakening of their own strategic position on the Eastern European front.

Had I not far more useful things to do currently, I could write a shelf of authoritative volumes on the weaknesses and errors of the Soviet and Eastern European economies and economic policies—beginning with the ulcer of Soviet agricultural history, and the worse mess in the almost feudalistic-relic organization of Polish agriculture. Yet, even if we consent, for the sake of present discussion, to the proposition that my criticisms might underestimate the weaknesses of the Soviet economy, the Soviet economy is by no means an overall net failure, nor is it about to collapse.

Quite the contrary. In extremely relevant areas of advanced physics, Soviet science is, overall, the most advanced in the world. The principal difficulty in this respect is that the Soviet ability to deploy its breakthroughs in scientific discovery is largely limited to a special section of its industry—its advanced military production facilities.

For the course of the 1980s, the Soviet economy's prospects are more favorable. In addition to having the largest number of qualified scientists of any nation, the science feature of Soviet primary and secondary school education has been forcefully improved since the middle 1960s, to the point that the emerging Soviet labor force will be the best qualified technologically in the world— especially considering the accelerating devolution in quality of educational content of the educational systems of all Atlantic Alliance nations over the comparable period to date. At some time during the course of the 1980s, excluding general war, the accumulation of combined scientific advances and technological potentials of the labor force as a whole will create the preconditions for a qualitative breakthrough in overall rates of Soviet economic performance, led by implications of forced breakthroughs in nuclear applications and related domains of advanced plasma physics.

Soviet attention to the relevant features of Riemann's development of Abelian functions is but one leading example of emerging qualitative advantages of Soviet over lagging Western science.

Of course, this evidence does not establish any sort of inherent superiority of the Soviet system over the industrial capitalist system. What it reflects, most essentially, is the damnable foolishness of those governments and other influentials of the West who have curtailed allocations for honest scientific research and development, and have tolerated the systematic destruction of quality in educational programs, especially since 1967. What it signifies for policy making, is not the superiority of the Soviet system, but rather the imperative of ridding educational programs of the influence of such sources as Jurgen Habermas, and putting priority on missive increases in allocations for nuclear energy development, scientific research laboratories, and high-technology capital investment generally.

Our essential strategic enemy is within. That enemy is the neo-Malthusian ideology associated with the Club of Rome, with those who oppose massive intelligence agency and law enforcement search-and-seal operations against national and international marijuana and other drug traffic, and associated with those superstitious influences echoing the tradition of Madame Blavatsky, Annie Besant, Teilhard de Chardin, the Huxleys, Margaret Mead, and Rudolf Steiner.

Finally, in connection with the same general theme, there are a few, irrational fanatics who insist that a leap in Atlantic Alliance military capabilities can be effected under conditions of the sort determined by the Carter administration's recently published "reindustrialization" program. The U.S. proponents of this wishful fanatic's absurdity, associated with such circles as George Bush's "Team B" collation of the Ford administration period, and with the likes of avowed neo-Malthusian James R. Schlesinger, have unfortunately succeeded in using their institutionalized positions of authority within the ranks of the Atlantic Alliance, to impel numerous more sensible people to adapt to such doctrines—essentially as a matter of craven submission to the imagined authority of the persons promulgating such nonsense.

One need but apply the appropriate bills of materials and production process sheets to the problem to prove how ludicrous the "guns not butter" proposition is. Such schemes cannot work, even if the task is delimited to achieving greater military capabilities in width. If one adds the requirement of seeking either parity or superiority in technologically advanced quality and depth, the "guns not butter" schemes currently afoot are in effect proposals to give Moscow victory in World War III by default.

Therefore, there is no rational basis in fact for the assumption that the application of the Thatcher model does not mean a commitment to inevitably growing strategic inferiority to the Soviet forces. Moreover, the very strategic desperation incited by such manifest trends, combined with the instabilities fostered by oppressive austerity and depression, means an increasingly unmanageable thrust toward the acts of strategic miscalculation adequate to trigger general nuclear war.

Notes

9. For later updated discussion of the implications of the Soviet actions fulfilling the spring 1979 prediction, see LaRouche, *Why Revival of SALT Won't Stop War* (New Benjamin Franklin House, 1980), pp. 3-5.

3

A New Monetary System

The present slide toward a new world depression leads toward what would be *potentially* the worst catastrophe European civilization has experienced since the "new dark age" of the early 14th century.

This trend is the result of, principally, two complementary causes. Broadly, the growing potential for an economic collapse, mediated by decay of the Bretton Woods monetary system, is the setting and broader objective cause for the present situation. However, those "objective" conditions are not the true cause of this situation. Influential Anglo-American political-financial circles, so far hegemonic in OECD monetary and energy policies, have chosen to foster and aggravate the onset of the potential new depression.

The less exotic side of the depression-choosing policy is adequately represented in a series of books compiled during 1975-1976 as the "1980s Project" of the New York Council on Foreign Relations (CFR)—the latter the principal U.S. daughter of the London Round Table and Royal Institute of International Affairs. The kernel of the policy matter is those documents' included proposal of a policy named "controlled disintegration," a policy of self-imposed economic collapse of both the OECD and emerging nations' economies, using monetary austerity measures as

Photo: Information Service of India

The ability of major developing nations to absorb capital goods exports, and replace poverty with modern productivity, is one primary objective of the National Democratic Policy Committee proposals for monetary reform. Above, India's Tarapur nuclear facility.

the pivotal mechanism for effecting such a general depression.[10]

The CFR authors' comprehension of the fact that they are choosing among two options is underlined by the rabid hatred of both Franco-German European Monetary System policies, and of the American System of political economy (Hamilton, List), set forth as an integral part of the recommendation of "controlled disintegration."

There is not a single policy thus far put forth by the U.S. Carter administration which was not set forth in either these CFR "1980s Project" books or in papers of the Trilateral

Commission circulated during the 1975-1976 period. In fact, Jimmy Carter is essentially the "puppet President" chosen to serve as the vehicle for putting these CFR-Trilateral-conduited policies into effect.

The more exotic, complementary aspect to this willful choosing of a new depression is typified by common ideological features of the Club of Rome, Blavatskyian theosophy-anthroposophy, and the "futurologist" ideological scenarios spun out by institutions including Stanford Research Institute, the latter one of numerous leading U.S. "daughters" of the London Tavistock Institute (Sussex). These cultish components of the Anglo-American current proposing the new depression differentiate themselves sharply from circles which embrace the Thatcher model merely as a purgative process preliminary to renewed economic progress.

The cultists, some leading portions of whom overtly describe themselves as a powerful "Aquarian Conspiracy,"[11] have adopted the goal of establishing the sort of Lucifer-worshiping "new dark age" utopia proposed —as a correlative of Lucifer worship!—by London-centered theosophical circles at the beginning of this century. That utopian perspective was given fresh energy during the 1920s and 1930s by such prominent leaders of British intelligence as H. G. Wells and Bertrand Russell, and furthered by such joint collaborators of Wells and Russell as Lucifer-cultist and psychedelist Aleister Crowley, and such Crowley confederates as the Huxley brothers and Jesuit cultist and hoaxster Teilhard de Chardin.[12]

The exotic cultists within the Anglo-American faction of the OECD's ruling elites are the dangerous fanatics involved, and the principal force behind environmentalist movements, international terrorism, and the notion of deploying the sodomizing, coprophiliac mullahs of "Islamic fundamentalism" as an instrument of policy against the government of Iran and other states of the Islamic world. This is the component of the OECD's policy-shaping elites which, in cooperation with the historically British-centered international opium-heroin traffickers, has launched a highly profitable, vast expansion of the drug traffic into OECD nations. This has been done as part of a program for destroying the minds and morals of large portions of youth, creating thus the "entry point" for assimilation into organized Lucifer-cultism as outlined in Teilhard de Chardin's elaboration of the theory of the "omega point."[13]

Consequently, in assessing the policy support for "controlled disintegration" today, we must distinguish between the two kinds of supporters of that policy, while recognizing that the "futurologist" element of cultism is, unfortunately, a significant constituent of the pro-controlled disintegration" forces as a whole.

Here, we address the rational component of the support for such a policy, having recorded our recognition of the existence of an influential additional, irrationalist source of support for the same short-term monetary-economic strategy.

Following the first major petroleum price crisis of 1973-1974, the Federal Republic of Germany devised and implemented most effective, offsetting programs of capital goods export promotion, whereas Gaullist France accelerated brilliantly its already founded nuclear energy programs. German export promotion not only strengthened the nation's balance-of-payments position directly. The main emphasis upon capital goods exports accelerated the rate of realized turnover of productive capital within the exporting industries of the Republic. This acceleration of turnover of productive capital invested in export industries and their vendors boosted the growth of effective productivity of the Republic's economy. So, the Republic not only used exports to cover the additional petroleum payment requirements incurred by 1973-1974 developments; it raised the average level of industrial productivity sufficiently to offset losses to effective productivity caused by increased energy prices.

German exports and France's accelerated nuclear programs combined to revive the industrial economies of continental Western Europe. The margin of exports from other continental European nations to the Federal Republic fostered principally by Germany's own capital goods exports programs, was the critical margin which accounts for the fact that, aided by the establishment of the new European Monetary System's first phase of operations, the founding EMS nations' industrial sectors achieved significant progress overall, in contrast to the accelerating collapse of the British, Canadian, and U.S. economies over the same period (1975-1979).

The continental Western European recovery was undermined by the combined effects of the U.S. "Volcker measures" initiated during early October 1979, and by the then impending, and soon implemented leaps in OPEC petroleum prices at the close of 1979. A crucial symptom of the consequence is Federal Republic data for March 1980. That month the rate of loss of overall productivity through increased energy prices overtook the compensating, ebbing upward movement in the Republic's productivity.

The effects on France are clear. The nation is being pushed into a recession. Although the Italian economy overall is a mess, a most unwholesome mess since the departure of the last Andreotti government and the establishment of the Piccoli-Craxi backed government of the present moment of writing, the industrial sub-sector of Italy's economy was previously viable, relative at least to the apparently insoluble bankruptcy of the Italian state. This industrial component of recovery within the Italian economy is now suffering visibly. When the Federal Republic's rate of growth of high-technology capital goods exports is depressed, all of continental Europe's economies suffer as a consequence.

There are three distinguishable, if interrelated elements directly depressing the Federal Republic's economy.

The first and most general is the effect of the combined collapse of the British and U.S. economies on the world market and the OECD economies in particular. The weight of these combined, collapsing sectors, plus the weight of the plunging U.S. dollar in world trade, means that a healthy Japan and relatively healthy continental Western Europe find it almost impossible to fend off the chain-reaction consequences of combined British and U.S. collapse, especially when this is compounded by continued rises in petroleum prices.

The second, directly U.S., contribution to depression of Europe's economies has been the "Volcker measures" effect on world financial markets. Volcker's high interest rates do not reduce the rate of inflation of the U.S. dollar. Directly the opposite. They increase the potential rate of monetary inflation savagely, up to the point that the impulse-rate of inflation is offset by outright depression rates of deflationary economic collapse.

Apart from the generally increased instability which the Volcker measures introduced to international monetary affairs, the counterproductive high interest rates imposed by Volcker, compounded by wild swings up and down in those rates since late spring, force Europe either to resort to some form of exchange-controls defense against Carter-Volcker madness, or to raise European interest rates defensively, to defend European financial markets against the effects of massive, purely speculative short-term outflows from Europe into U.S. financial markets. This defensive action exports the depressive effects of the

Volcker measures from Britain and the United States into the economies of continental Western Europe—in addition to being a monstrous disaster for the economies of emerging nations.

The inflationary spiral in effective borrowing costs so accelerated, produces a degree of debt management crisis in even the most promising emerging-nation capital goods markets. Fostering of "hot spots" in the Middle East, through combined effect of the Carter administration's "Camp David" dogmas and schemes for destabilizing the Persian Gulf region as a whole, dries up the last remaining principal European "Third World" export markets but for the Comecon nations. The orchestration of the Polish crises by Anglo- American-led intelligence networks is the leading edge of a series of measures designed to destroy continental Western Europe's Comecon trade relations as well.

Beyond the monetary and economic effects of these developments and trends, worse measures are in store.

Every leading financier-insider's and related circle's reports have prediscounted a projected imminent collapse of export levels from the Gulf region, anticipating a collapse to occur by as early as November of this present year. Anglo-American factions have in place an operation-scenario designed to topple the Saudi royal family, with aid of "Islamic fundamentalist" mullahs and their crazed, superstitious dupes. The emplacement of the U.S. "rapid deployment force" into the Indian Ocean region represents variously a complementary, or alternative scenario-potential for effecting drastic cuts in Middle East petroleum production. *This means, of course, a probable doubling of world market petroleum prices above current rates.*

The Carter administration has also openly prediscounted such a development. While continuing to sabotage nuclear energy development, with aid of an entirely hypocritical "non- proliferation" doctrine, it has proposed the creation of a "Copec" cartel, centered upon nations including the United States and Australia. The object is to do to the world's economy with skyrocketing, monopolist coal prices what was done, under the direction of the London petroleum marketing cartel, with petroleum prices.

In addition, it is estimated that a per barrel price for petroleum significantly above $60 is the lower limit for competitive production of "synfuel" using the relatively archaic (Auschwitz-copied) modes presently adopted as policy by the Carter administration.

Complementing this transformation of the United States into part of a "Copec" monopoly, the Carter administration has adopted a so-called reindustrialization program which would eliminate numerous categories of U.S. basic industry, reduce U.S. food production by more than one-third, and "triage" savagely other categories of productive output. Coal, synfuel, and Brzezinski's list of "technetronic" industries would be, in addition to legalized mass drug addiction, whorehouses and other forms of recreational "services," the few relatively prosperous industries amid a nation of Americans largely reduced to relative conditions of servitude in labor-intensive employment at marginal wages.

Without assuming that Carter's monstrous scheme would actually go into effect in exactly the terms he and DuPont's "Hermann Goering," Irving Shapiro, have recently proposed, it is sufficient to project the kinds of conditions resulting from the effort to impose anything resembling such a program under conditions of the onset of a new general depression. The effects must necessarily compare with those of the early fourteenth century's "new dark ages."

However, nothing in human policy making is truly inevitable beforehand, except as man-made policies, or the want of suitable such policies, dictate the unchecked onset of calamities such as great depressions. This new depression is in no sense "objectively inevitable." There is no "factor" so potent that it could not be overcome—even at this late date, if the political will to implement the right policy choices were found among a few OECD nations' governments.

The proof is elementary. If we brush from our minds the fog of popularized monetary dogmas, it is evident that supplying the educated and otherwise relatively literate urban populations of developing nations with state-of-the-art capital goods, we can put the unemployed of such strata to work, and raise by an order of magnitude the per capita output of those who are already employed in a relatively labor-intensive way. Even in areas in which farmers are illiterate, but otherwise essentially good farmers, the well-managed provision of irrigation, fertilizers, improved strains and so forth, can increase both per hectare and per capita output substantially more than the costs of production are increased by the new inputs. Hence, forgetting monetary dogmas for a moment, and looking at the matter in strictly economics-of-production terms, there is no doubt among sane men and women that a massive potential exists for generating a global capital exports boom from the industrialized nations. On condition that the schedule of payments for these capital goods infusions is shaped to correspond with the development of the buyer's increased ability to pay, as if in barter terms, the capital goods boom so projected is unquestionably a sound, presently existent potential.

Within the OECD countries themselves, the simple recognition that sociologists, as sociologists, are intrinsically parasites would spearhead a reexamination of the merits of categories of labor-intensive services occupations more generally. By putting parasitically employed service categories to useful work, using modern productive technologies, we would reduce considerably the monstrous factor of overhead waste in these economies, while increasing the average amount of wealth produced for the nations as a whole. Given appropriate productive employment, even a sociologist can produce significantly more than he or she presently gobbles from the trough of the *Sozialmarktwirtschaft*, and can thus be transformed from a menace into a respectable, productive citizen.

The secret of overcoming a depression under this sort of circumstance is essentially the following. Instead of proceeding from the misassumption that monetary orders are the essential reality of economies, and that production and consumption must therefore submit to the conditions demanded by an existing monetary order, reverse one's approach. *Design a monetary system whose mechanisms are enslaved to the requirements of profitable economic growth, as measured in terms of the input-output relations of the productive process as such.*

We cannot propose to do quite exactly that, in point of fact. We could, in principle, nullify all existing financial debts and assets, and construct a new financial order from the base of the requirements of the economic (non-monetary) foundations. However, resort to such drastic action means collapsing existing banking and many other institutions.

A middle road must be discovered and chosen. Without undermining the integrity of existing financial structures, we must steer the operations of those institutions into new directions, while at the same time establishing durable value for a mass of financial paper which is now, on the whole, rotting around the edges.

The classic policy discussion relevant to the proposal just outlined is the extended discussion of the reorganization of the United States' debt submitted to the Congress of the first George Washington administration by Treasury Secretary Alexander Hamilton. The reasons for the debtor's fully honoring the old debts, in establishing an entirely new U.S. banking and monetary order, are those which would be acceptable to every sensible banker in the world today, and should be equally acceptable, both on moral and practical grounds, to the overwhelming majority of the nation's citizens. The principle of *equity*, the cornerstone of the civil law of European civilization, is fully served.

Starting from an understanding of the kind of new monetary system, we must apply the notion of that new monetary system to the problem of reorganizing the system of credit as it exists under the monetary-financial order of the present moment. The transition from the present state of affairs to that we must reach a generation hence is constructed by means of gold-denominated, rediscountable long-term bonds. Thus, old debts are converted into the form of a long-term, currently usable financial asset, while the repayment of those instruments is deferred to a time of the debtor's enhanced ability to pay.

There are several ways in which the OECD nations could immediately establish the sort of new world monetary system needed to halt this depression. However, all workable such alternatives would coincide in principled features with the following step-by-step outline. No other variety of measures could succeed—without discarding the principle of equity identified above.

The optimal first step would be a treaty agreement between the President of the United States and the nations of the European Monetary System. This agreement would peg the monetary gold price at a level, probably denominated in the value of ECUs[14] at the time of the agreement, which corresponded to the purchase of mined new stocks of monetary gold at prices consistent with an average rate of profit to gold producers. The monetary gold stocks of the U.S., the largest of any nation, would be pledged as U.S. purchase of partnership in *a new, gold-reserve-based international rediscount institution* established on the cornerstone of implementation of "Phase Two" of the European Monetary System.

The initial action of the new rediscount institution would be essentially an internal transaction among the national treasuries, central banks and participating private banks of the new monetary partnership.

The new institution would issue a series of long-term bonds, denominated in gold-pegged ECUs, and bearing a highly competitive yield of between 2 and 3 percent. These bonds would soak up excess dollar obligations, plus a selected mixture of other currencies. These bonds, purchased by treasuries, central banks, private banks, and certain other appropriate kinds of institutions, would be discountable with the rediscount facility for purposes of securing participation credit for approved categories of hard-commodity lending.

The next preparatory step is matching action by indebted Third World nations. (We exclude, for the moment, the special category of so-called least-developed nations.) These nations would issue a series of long-term, gold-ECU-denominated bonds, bearing a nominal yield, and with deferred payment coupon provisions as appropriate. These bonds would be discountable with the new rediscount facility on the same basis as the regular bonds of that facility.

These bonds would be used to purchase outstanding debt held by financial institutions participating in the new monetary partnership.

Where appropriate such institutions do not yet exist, the Third World nations involved will qualify to participate in such rescheduling arrangements by either establishing a suitable form of "national development bank," or participating in a "regional development bank" serving a group of nations. Such banks will be the issuers of the bonds endorsed by the national treasuries of the nations represented. Crucial in this feature is the necessity of maintaining the integrity of the rule of lending new hard-commodity credit, by establishing banking institutions which bind themselves by treaty to the same principles of credit utilization as adopted by the new international rediscount institution.

It is permissible to consolidate a mass of carried-over indebtedness under one package of initial issue of the new class of bonds. However, respecting the further incurring of debt in the form of new issues of such bonds, the rules of hard-commodity lending adopted by the new monetary system must be strictly adhered to.

The general object is to generate a base for between two and four hundred billion dollars-equivalent of new hard-commodity credit issuance annually. This new credit should be restricted to the following preconditions for lending:

1)   Medium- to long-term credit for intrinsically profitable industrial, agricultural productive investments, plus *high-technology-only* energy production, water systems, and transportation systems within developing nations.

2) Construction loans and hard-commodity international trade credit in support of approved developmental investments of borrowing developing nations.

3) Operating capital and production capacity credit to firms of OECD nations against delivery of hard-commodity output to approved development projects of developing nations.

4) Considerations of performance capability and credit worthiness of end-borrowers of both developing and OECD nations.

The projected price of credit extended by the new rediscount institution is between 4 percent and 6 percent, denominated in gold-ECU terms. In general, this credit shall be issued as a percentile of participation in the entirety of a loan, other participation provided as private bank credit, governmental loans, and so forth.

Outstanding Technical Objections to Such Measures

The only durable objections to such actions from the ranks of qualified bankers and like categories would be *ideological objections*. There would be some notable fuss about the undermining of the present roles of the International Monetary Fund, World Bank, and Basel private Bank of International Settlements. Considering the successful proselytizing among bankers by the Mont Pelerin Society's monetarists, there would be loud objections to the "dirigist" character of the proposed new credit arrangements.

Technically, it would be possible—at least, in abstraction—to revise the articles of the International Monetary Fund to the effect of transforming it into the new, gold-reserve-based international rediscount facility required. I have no principled objection to doing that, if it could be done in fact. I admit, furthermore, that such a course of action seems to possess the advantage of offering a kind of path of least resistance to monetary reform. Many of my friends in France appear to be inclined to that view at present. I admit that it is desirable to explore the possibility of reforming existing, well-established institutions, since such options, if workable, minimize the "institutional shock" and resistance set into motion, and may thus be a means for getting the job done with a minimization of institutional shocks.

It happens, in my considered view, that the IMF, World Bank, and BIS bureaucracies are so habituated to the old ways of doing things that it would be better to start fresh with a new institution, than to attempt to reeducate the hardened bureaucracies of the old.

If a compromise exists between the two alternatives, I propose that it is to be found in establishing a relationship between a reformed IMF and the brand new international rediscount institution.

That, I believe, is my adequate response to the cited form of first, institutional objection to the proposal for the new rediscount facility. We turn now to a more extended evaluation of the anti-dirigist ideology underlying the second class of objections.

Exemplary of the ideological problem, there is a linguist's hoax currently popular in the Federal Republic of Germany. Some industrious heirs of Bertrand Russell's and Karl Korsch's founding of radical-nominalist "linguistics," have perpetrated a prank of mental torture upon many of the people of that nation. The gist of the prank is this: a purely legendary *Freimarktwirtschaft* has been counterposed to an equally apocryphal *Sozialmarktwirtschaft*. Often enough, the debates centered around those non-existent entities remind one of metaphysical practices of the late thirteenth and early fourteenth century University of Paris.

Obviously, the practical effect of such debates over non-existent entities is to divert attention from real issues. It is this diversion which is the real effect of the ideological debate. In that way, and in only that fashion, a certain, perverted kind of real value comes to be associated with what were, originally, terms for merely fictional existences.

The way in which the hoax has functioned is as follows. Predominantly, anti-socialist prejudice is cathexized to the otherwise empty word, *Freimarktwirtschaft*, while more liberal to socialist prejudices are attached, defensively, to the otherwise empty word, *Sozialmarktwirtschaft*. The effect of such "belief-structure" conditioning of the population is to make the originally empty word, *Freimarktwirtschaft*, synonymous with "capitalism." In addition, a purely ideological play on the words "free" and "capitalism," coupled in such a merely nominalist fashion, renders a superstitious view of *Freimarktwirtschaft* more or less synonymous with a "bulwark against bolshevism."

By this sort of linguistician's trickery, both defenders and opponents of the term *Freimarktwirtschaft* are conditioned to equating "freedom" and "capitalism" with those "free trade" policies of Adam Smith's employer, the British East India Company. Those are the "free trade" policies against which the American Revolution was fought, and *against which leading German republicans, including von Cotta and List, fought, in establishing the German Zollverein and initiating other dirigist (anti-"free trade") programs for development of Germany's coal, metals, chemicals and railway industries.*

Under the auspices of such trickery, currents such as those of the Mont Pelerin Society advance a curious sort of doctrine of "economic freedom." It is curious even at first inspection, since Professor Milton Friedman, the leading

U.S. Mont Pelerinite spokesman, insists that the present military government of Chile and the Hong Kong heroin capital are two among the leading examples of relative such "economic freedom" at present. This perversity in the use of the term "freedom" continues as we explore the doctrine in greater depth.

The Mont Pelerinites' notion of "freedom" centers around the following leading elements of belief structure. There must be no regulation of business affairs by the state. However, the leading financial institutions, thus left unencumbered by the authority of the state, are advised to impose crushing austerity on the state, and to resort to economic dictatorship in detail, through such vehicles as the "conditionalities" doctrine of the International Monetary Fund. That is a most curious understanding of the term "freedom"!

Thus, under the influence of such doctrines we are instructed that it is correct, even mandatory, to impose monetary-economic dictatorship to the point of causing mass deaths by famine and epidemic throughout much of the world, as well as brutal economic hardship upon many in the OECD nations. Otherwise, we are similarly instructed, it would be an unacceptable interference in the "free market" to propose to regulate the flows of centralized credit, to act to favor productive categories of investment over pure speculation and gambling casinos.

The further, directly contrasting observation to be recorded on this matter is that most among the persons who tolerate such policies are otherwise rational, intelligent, and include very capable financial and industrial leaders.

There are several contributing features of the current environment to be considered.

First, respecting widespread preference for a dictatorship by finance over nations and national governments, most OECD (and other) governments have earned contempt over most of the postwar period to date. Although President Charles de Gaulle was a notable exception to this, and although Adenauer, Giscard and Schmidt have earned the relatively highest marks for crisis-management and statesmanship among OECD governments generally, the quality of the leading parties of the OECD (and many other nations) has been declining at an alarming rate over the past fifteen years.

Granting that Franz-Josef Strauss has relatively exceptional capabilities as a politician, Chancellor Helmut Schmidt stands out in performance far above most of the other choices of leaders of all the parties. This situation in Germany and other nations is not accidental. The quality of politicians being developed, generally, by the leading parties of the OECD nations is constantly becoming poorer. The tendency toward William James's concoction of "pluralism" requires intellectual and moral mediocrity among its supporters, and induces mediocrity even among political figures who might have developed as competent statesmen under better circumstances. With a relative handful of exceptional figures noted, the very name "politician" has become justly synonymous with bungling and incompetence.

Of course, as an American, I admit that the situation in the United States is relatively the worst for any OECD nation on this account.

Hence, there is a discreetly unspoken policy among numerous leading bankers, industrialists, and so forth. "We had better keep the politicians out of monetary and economic policy. Those bunglers would only make a mess of everything.

Second, the Mont Pelerin Society sort of policy outlook has been superimposed upon many leading figures under peer-group pressure.

Third, there are virtually no policy-formulating institutions, involving leaders of finance, industry, trade unions, scientists and political figures, which have been employed in seeking to discover and elaborate policies alternate to those emanating from leading Anglo-American think tanks. Many accept Mont Pelerinist outlooks, because no elaborated alternative has been introduced into the organic life of leading financial, industrial, etc. circles. This point will be summarily treated in the conclusion of this report.

Finally, according to all evidence in sight, there is not a single university of the OECD nations which has offered a competent course in economics during the postwar period. Worse, there is not only a virtual suppression of all of the essential facts of modern economic history, but what is offered as economic historiography in available textbooks and in the published output of the so-called economic experts is chiefly outright fiction, falsification.

Consider the impact of this spread of incompetent economic dogmas upon the leading industrialist, for example. As an industrialist, this figure has a working grasp of the input-output relations of production of wealth, and a grasp of the way in which advances in energy flux density and improved capital-intensive technology promote advances in productivity, as well as enlarging the scale of real wealth of societies. However, when this person's focus is shifted away from the area of industrial management in particular, to matters of national and global monetary policy, the industrial leader's competence usually is more or less pushed to one side—up to the point that a monetarist-designed proposal is perceived to conflict directly with the vital interests of some section of industry. This leader is usually awed into intellectual submission by the mere attachment of an arbitrary title of "professional expertise" to a kind of monetarist economic dogma which is in fact dangerous gobbledygook.

The summarized highlights of the history of industrial capitalism are outlined here, to illustrate the nature of what is not known to most leading circles today.

The development of industrial capitalism has two principal aspects and corresponding phases.

The first of these is the establishment of the modern nation-state itself, a new institution first realized under

France's Louis XI and England's Henry VII, at the close of the fifteenth century. This conception of the modern nation-state republic, known as the commonwealth to sixteenth and seventeenth century England and France, was modeled on the policy adduced from Plato's writings, and was defined as a continuation of the ancient city-builders' dedication to science and technological progress.

The second leading aspect of the development of modern industrial capitalism was first well defined during the second half of the seventeenth century. The crucial fact of this development was the continuity expressed by the work of both Jean-Baptiste Colbert and Colbert's titanic protégé Gottfried Wilhelm Leibniz. As distinct from the branch of pseudo-political economy launched by William Petty in Britain, *Leibniz is uniquely the founder of systematic modern scientific political economy.*

It must be emphasized that Leibniz's notion of political economy is not merely opposite axiomatically to every distinguishing feature of the British and Vienna schools. For Leibniz, fundamental scientific progress, technological progress, development of production, promotion of commerce, military science, and the process of economic growth through realized productive investment of profits are all one subject of scientific statecraft, of nation-building. Felix Klein's Göttingen Verein was a useful, if diluted echo of the continuation of Leibniz's methods of nation-building, through Halle into Göttingen, most notably.

In France, the same current represented by Leibniz in Germany was centered around the Oratorian Catholic order, the leading French Catholic political opposition to the Jesuit order. (The Oratorians were disbanded by the Jesuit-"liberation theology"-created Jacobins during the 1790s.) In France, the work of Leibniz and his collaborators reached a high-point of revitalization under the leadership of Oratorian-trained Gaspard Monge and Lazare Carnot, through such media as the development of the Ecole Polytechnique. Although the Jesuit's agent Augustin Cauchy, among others, nearly destroyed the leading influence of the Monge-Carnot school (e.g., Legendre) in France during the later nineteenth century, the most essential of the contributions of the Monge-Carnot group were directly assimilated by Göttingen-centered heirs of Leibniz in Germany. The personalities of Weierstrass, Riemann and Cantor are outstanding on this account.

It was the Leibniz policy of political economy, originally and most emphatically transmitted from the French heirs of Colbert, which defined the political-economic principles of the majority of leading forces in the American Revolution (e.g., Franklin, Washington, Hamilton, Mathew Carey, et al.). The system of credit, national banking, and promotion of manufactures which came to be known internationally as the American System, was a French-developed policy mediated into U.S. constitutional law with aid of such vehicles as Treasury Secretary Alexander Hamilton's policy outlines of the first George Washington administration.

These policies, although sabotaged substantially by British-influenced Jefferson and Madison, were advanced by leaders within the Cincinnatus Society, and by the joint, close collaborator of Franklin's and Hamilton's, Mathew Carey.

The further elaboration of the scientific principles of Colbert-Leibniz political economy was accomplished under the leadership of Monge and Carnot, especially in the work of Claude Chaptal and, later, Charles A. Dupin—the latter the fictionalized hero of the Edgar Allan Poe detective stories. Both the American and French aspects of this continuation of Leibnizian economics were integrated by a leading German republican protégé of the Marquis de Lafayette, Friedrich List.

It was List who made Hamilton's term "American System" an international by-word. It was the revival of American System policies under U.S. presidents Monroe, John Quincy Adams, and Lincoln which made the names of Hamilton, Carey, and List the by-words of the adoption of the American System by the Meiji Restoration in Japan. It was the American System in this form which was used by German republicans to foster the combined development of the metals, chemicals and railway industries in Germany, together with the development of mining and powered river commerce.

Therefore, to propose that the anti-American System British doctrine of "free trade" can be equated directly to the development of industrial capitalism is historically utter nonsense, premised upon sweeping ignorance of the history of capitalist development.

Moreover, if one studies the polemical attacks exchanged between the respective supporters of the British and French-German-American-Japanese system of industrial capitalist development over the course of the 19th century, a rational person is obliged to concede that it is the American System, as associated with Hamilton, Carey and List, which is the consistent doctrine of industrial capitalist self-interest, whereas, as Carey and List, among others, emphasize, the British System is essentially the superimposition of "feudalist" forms of rentier-monetarist rule upon a subordinated, looted industrial capitalist, plus colonial basis beneath.

The function of "free trade" policies is to use a fostering of anarchic competition as a means for reducing to a minimum the prices of manufactured and agricultural products. This, in turn, causes a massive relative depression of wages of operatives employed in industry and on farms. The producing classes of capitalist society—the industrialists, the farmers, the productive operatives employed—are forced to accept reduced incomes. The result is a concentration of a greater portion of the wealth produced by the economy in the hands of a rentier-financier cartel and its oligarchical partners in state power.

The elaboration of that British system of "free trade" is efficiently studied by focusing attention initially on the introduction of large-scale "tax farming" practices with the 1603 accession of James I to the united kingdoms of Great

Britain. Britain was turned over, economically, to the looting activities of a cartel of Venice-Genoa-Geneva-Amsterdam financiers, through principally the Amsterdam channel across the North Sea, and by way of "offshore," Genoa-allied financial interests centered around Edinburgh. As Britain developed a position of primus inter pares among the Venice-Genoa "black nobility"-spawned rentier cartel, especially after the early 1770s crisis of the Amsterdam and Geneva banks, it was the Scottish border forces, the Genoa-linked "offshore" banks centered around Edinburgh, which established their subsequent long rule over Britain, through the medium of their special creation, the British East India Company. East India Company protégé Adam Smith was promoted simply as a kind of "Josef Goebbels" for the policy which Britain followed in the 1776-1783 war against the Americans.

An opposing case is found, not only in the history of periodic employment of national banking policies by the United States. The financing of Japan's trading companies operations, and the distinctive points of qualitative superiority of German banking over British banking in developing industry help to enrich one's comprehension of the real issues involved.

Conceding all the various complications of German financial and economic history since the establishment of the Zollverein, we isolate from this the most interesting and commendable feature of German private banking, the relationship between those banks and the German industrial firms. It is the ability of powerful, technologically progressive, and profitable industrial firms to deliver exemplary performance in large-scale export of capital goods, as well as domestic capital formation, which fosters the strength of the bankers allied with such firms.

Under favorable circumstances of that sort, banks are able to function more emphatically as venture-capital bankers, whether in their capacity as organizers of risk-capital equity investments, or as extenders of medium-to-long-term investment credit and export credits.

The consistent policy of the Neoplatonic forces behind the emergence of the modern industrial capitalist form of sovereign nation-state, including France's Louis XI and England's Henry VII, has been Colbertist: to establish a state which would promote fair trade in a fostering of commerce, and thus generate profitable levels of commerce in products of industry and farms. Such profitable commerce promotes those advances in real wages of the productive labor force which are indispensable for raising the level of culture of the labor force in a manner consistent with technological progress, (as well as the cultural requirements of citizenship generally). This profitability, in turn, promotes increasingly capital-intensive, technologically progressive investment for sustained improvements in the productivity of industry and agriculture.

The proper policy of the state is to intervene in overall commerce, to aid in maintaining fair prices for products of industry and agriculture, and thus make possible advances in wage levels and culture of the general population. It must also be the policy and action of the state to ensure that the majority of the economic surplus produced by society is concentrated in the form of reinvestible profits of industry, agriculture, and related enterprises. The state's taxation and credit policies create the incentives which reward productive reinvestment of profits, and which penalize, even to the point of cruelty, the failure to reinvest earned portions of the nation's economic surplus productively.

A competent industrial capitalist policy is a Colbertist policy, *a dirigist policy*.

In the false propaganda of the defenders of the British system, dirigism is equated, mythologically, to the draconian form of bureaucratic regulation of the details of economic life typified by wartime controls. It is in this setting that such variously miseducated or even lying ideologues attempt to equate the dirigist character of the American System morally with Soviet statism.

Contrary to such combined impressions and false propaganda, the dirigist industrial-capitalist state properly emphasizes the decisive importance of individual creative initiative. *The ultimate source of all real wealth of society is the contributions effected through the development of the creative powers of the individual.* This is both the power to effect scientific and subsumed forms of discovery respecting the lawful ordering of the universe, and what Clausewitz gropes clumsily to identify in his discussion of *Entschlossenheit*:   the power to see through the implementation of a discovery in practice, to make the implementation successful under conditions others may be impotently considering such action a mere theoretical possibility. Therefore, we properly emphasize not only formal qualities of individual creative potentials as such, but also the executive qualities of initiative which translate insight into a realized accomplishment. For simplification, we may prefer to use the term "individual creative initiative."

Such individual creative initiative is synonymous with the idea of "freedom" properly conceived.

Therefore, although the modern industrial capitalist state may be obliged to undertake directly certain large-scale productive and infrastructural investments, beyond the means of individual firms singly or collectively, the modern state abhors properly state bureaucratic intervention into the *isolable details* of internal economic life. The principal economic and related actions of the state are, apart from certain large-scale investments, properly limited to shaping the whole "outer" environment of individual economic practice: by national tariff and trade policies, by national banking and credit policies, and by taxation policies. The economic function of the state is to establish and protect *an environment for* economic creative initiative by individuals and groups of individuals.

Conversely, the Marxian portrayal of the "business cycle" does not represent, in fact, a phenomenon intrinsic to industrial capitalism. It is, rather, a disorder endemic to the British system of "free trade."

The key to Marx's axiomatic error on this point is his credulous acceptance of the British model as the exemplar of industrial capitalist forms. It is the discouraging of investment in new productivities, largely as a consequence of anarchically competitive depression of producers' prices (and, in chain-reaction consequence, of real wage rates), and the flow of investments into relatively spiraling masses of indebtedness, analogous economically to tax-farming indebtedness, which causes the lagging of productive investment, accompanied by spiraling debt-equity ratios, which are the direct cause both of monetary inflation and of the deflationary plunges triggered by such inflation.

If the proportion of total economic surplus concentrated as producer's profits and household savings is kept very high, and if scientific and technological progress are fostered sufficiently, no capitalist economy so ordered could ever generate "business cycle" phenomena of the sort outlined in Marx's *Capital*. Or, a corrollary of the same point, Marx's sort of business-cycle collapses occur only where British political-economic doctrines of "free trade" predominate.

The complementary, opposing current associated with the scholastic form of debate over *Freimarktwirtschaft* versus *Sozialmarktwirtschaft*, is the left-wing social-democratic or ultra-liberal sorts of opposition to industrial capitalist political economy.

The prevailing contemporary British and Vienna-school doctrines of political economy are not essentially derivatives of studies of actual economic processes. They are as John Stuart Mill, Jevons and others declare themselves on this point. They are outgrowths of the doctrine of "hedonistic calculus" associated with Jeremy Bentham, and also with Bentham's "utilitarian" successors, in furthering that Benthamite "felicific calculus." This sort of Benthamite liberalism, sometimes termed more rigorously "British philosophical radicalism," is the basis for the so-called left-wing extremist misconceptions of economic policy, and hence the origin of the left-wingers' efforts to import meaning to the otherwise empty category of *Sozialmarktwirtschaft*.

In real, scientific political economy of the sort flowing from the seminal work of Leibniz, the social valuation of a produced object is determined by the way in which the capital or household consumption of that object regenerates new productive capacities, outputs, and productive powers of members of households. This view of economic value, that of the American System economists, of Dupin, et al., leads to the analysis of economic processes over time as thermohydrodynamic processes, as we do in the case of the LaRouche-Riemann Model. We judge the momentary output of production as representing a *degree of regenerative potential*.

In the hedonistic-empiricist schools of Britain and Vienna, the gratification of the individual consumer *psychologically* by the sensuous act of consumption is the end point of the economic process. Everything produced simply vanishes externally into the maws of variegated forms of psychological gluttony. It is the pleasure and pain associated with isolated features of the productive process, and with the consumption of products or services, which is the axiomatic, exclusive basis for those British and Vienna varieties of hedonistic-empiricist doctrines: Mill, Jevons, Marshall, Keynes, and the postwar Mont Pelerin Society.

Left-wing pseudo-economics proposes that the ruling criteria for state economic policies are sufficiently established by the current assortment of episodic hedonistic preferences of the population. The doctrine of "pluralism," invented by the American British agent-of-influence William James at the close of the 19th century, is the political correlative of left-wing hedonistic pseudo-economics.

The "mullahs" of left-wing pseudo-economics not only deny the existence of a knowable rationality in the self-development of the economic process; they denounce every effort to judge hedonistic impulses and political policy judgments by any consistently rational criteria variously as "oppression," as "elitist," or "authoritarian."

In the view offered by such left-wingers, if a significant minority is offended by nuclear energy production, or by the present level of economic progress generally, then society must compromise with those unwashed wretches, by adapting to the demand for a degree of economic devolution. Such a policy means the genocidal death of billions of persons, if made the policy of the majority of the OECD nations. Nevertheless, according to the mixture of left-wing pseudo-economics and the irrationalists' doctrine of "pluralism," such mass murder of billions is morally obligatory, simply because a minority of "environmentalist mullahs" demands it.

It is the adaptation of state economic policy to left-wing pressures of that sort which imparts a nauseating component to the reputation of *Sozialmarktwirtschaft*.

An Example: The Case of Agriculture

Before proceeding from this issue, to our second principal point, the principles of credit generation, our foregoing arguments for governmental tariff and trade policies should be made more concrete for the reader. The principles involved are adequately illustrated by considering a leading issue between the majority of the Common Market community and Britain, the issue of agricultural parity prices.

For this purpose, we summarize the case for U.S. agriculture.

Beginning with the onset of the Second World War, the U.S. Roosevelt administration employed memory of U.S. agricultural policy from the period of the First World War, to effect a rapid recovery of U.S. farming generally. Essentially, U.S. farmers were assured a targeted market volume, and were assured parity prices for farm products.

A parity price for U.S. agriculture is most efficiently calculated in the following general manner.

In practice, the development of a calculated parity price for agricultural products proceeds by the following steps.

Eliminating the data peculiar to the relatively poorest performance farms and also the most productive small fraction of total farming, assemble estimated standard costs. These are properly compiled, first, in industrial engineering forms of standard bills of materials and process-analysis data. Secondly, these bills of materials and process-analysis data are extended for unit price per element of the cost analysis.

To this competitive average cost, we must add the capital cost represented by improved land, and also a standard factor for farmer's income. To this must be added an operating profit, which covers debt-service requirements plus a net operating farmers' profit, at a competitive rate of return on investment.

This determines the parity price at which the economy will be able to maintain not only a constant level of such output, but maintain some definable approximate rate of technological (productivity) progress.

The sophistry usually advanced against such parity pricing policy is that it results in an increased cost of food to consumers, in excess of a "free trade" competitive price. We shall refute that incompetent argument for "free trade," after briefly reviewing the effects of the U.S. government's drift away from a parity price policy, a drift which began under the last years of the U.S. Truman administration.

As a consequence of the government's abandoning a parity policy for agricultural products, beginning the early 1950s, the U.S. farmers have, on the average, operated at

an operating loss over each of most of the past 30 years!
To produce a product sold at a price less than the cost of
producing it, means to trade away some combination of
fixed capital and even also part of operating capital
investment in agriculture.

For those who profess to be incredulous at this report,
we supply the following additional, most relevant
information.

Over most of this period, a speculatively determined
market price for most agricultural land has boosted the
nominal value of the farmer's land. This speculative
inflation of farm land prices has emerged over the period as
the most important technical-financial consideration
feeding a spiraling of per hectare agricultural indebtedness.
In other words, the farmer who lost productive capital
through below parity prices of his sold product, replaced
and sometimes also augmented the lost portion of that
capital with borrowed capital. Such loans were often in
fairly abundant supply, and in parts, at relatively low
borrowing costs. In sum, the independent American farmer
—the most productive farmer in the world—stayed in
business by mortgaging out his farm.

That the current price for agricultural land (among most
other real estate) is purely speculative, is proven by treating
the debt service incurred from mortgaging out this land as
economic rent. How many years of operating income from
agricultural production on that land would be required to
purchase that land, even under conditions of parity prices
for agricultural products?

Clearly, the prevailing agricultural policies of the U.S. government over most of the past three decades have been increasingly economically *insane!*

Complementing the problems caused for the domestic U.S. economy by recent U.S. governments' agricultural dogmas, let us shift our attention for a moment to the world market. Over most of the postwar period, the agricultural exporting powers of the world, notably the United States and key British Commonwealth nations, have been in effect dumping agricultural products on the world market. This depression of the world market price for agricultural products prevents the development of profitable margins of operating income for food production among developing nations and certain other nations. The resulting lack of flow of investment and loan capital into the technological development of agriculture is the bleeding ulcer of many developing nations' economies, and the source of an emerging world food shortage.

The "free-traders" throw up their hands in horror. We propose to raise food prices? Over the short run, we do propose *to increase the prices paid to farmers.* That, however, is a small part of the total cost of food sold to consumers overall. Over the medium-to-long term, we will be reducing food prices considerably. While keeping the net operating profits for agricultural investment high, we propose to reduce the farmer's unit cost of production, through capital improvements in agricultural technology.

By providing prices which leverage flows of investment and loan capital into development of agriculture, we increase capital-intensive development of agricultural productivity. That is the only possible way in which to reduce the cost of food, and therefore the only way in which food prices can be reduced without creating murderous food shortages.

Therefore, sensible governments will join forces to establish a network of tariff and trade agreements which ensure a world parity price for agricultural products within the volumes estimated as required. By creating national and international agencies which intervene into the markets to which farmers sell, to make inventory purchases which keep the market orderly at parity prices, and by selling those inventories which are in excess of strategic food reserves on the world market at treaty-prices, governments establish the market conditions under which the free creative initiatives of individual farmers will accomplish most of the rest.

To repeat the point: It is not by intervening into the internal market in detail that government properly directs the healthy development of economy overall. There are essentially four areas of proper government intervention:

(1) Domestic and foreign tariff and trade policy, as illustrated by the discussion of agricultural parity price.

(2) National monetary and credit policy, including a policy of selectively favoring high-technology productive uses of the main flows of credit over marginally productive and non-productive uses.

(3) National taxation policy, giving very substantial after-tax income advantages to those firms, farms *and households* which invest in high-technology, capital-intensive productive investment, and relative tax penalties for those who do not.

(4) A limited range of governmental direct sponsorship of state economic projects, especially essential works beyond the capability of private firms.

Provided these four-fold state dirigist policies are maintained for practice in a climate of fostering of both scientific and technological progress, and a science-biased compulsory public educational program for the labor force generally, a "directed" economy will tend to perform excellently with a minimum of corrective sorts of exceptional interventions by the state.

Notes

10. Cf. Lyndon H. LaRouche, Jr., *Will the Soviets Rule in the 1980s?* (New York: New Benjamin Franklin House, 1979). The opening chapter reviews relevant policies of the New York Council on Foreign Relations' 1975-1976 "1980s Project" policy outlines for the incoming Carter administration.

11. Marilyn Ferguson, *The Aquarian Conspiracy* (Los Angeles: J. P. Tarcher, 1980).

12. Carol White, *The New Dark Ages Conspiracy* (New York: New Benjamin Franklin House, 1980),

passim. The first open proposal for launching a cultist-utopian "Age of Aquarius" was associated with Britain's Aleister Crowley, at the beginning of the present century. At the time, the proposal to make "Lucifer" the central figure of religious worship for the "Age of Aquarius" was associated not only with the Isis-Urania cult headed by Crowley, but with the Blavatskyian theosophists and the anthroposophical spinoffs.

13. Cf. Ferguson, op. cit.

14. The European Currency Unit (ECU), established in 1978 in association with the European Monetary System, has been the vehicle for the phased remonetization of gold holdings of European nations since that time. The ECU is not itself a single currency but a numeraire for a basket of the currencies of the member-nations of the European Monetary System. Credit denominated in gold-pegged ECUs is transferred in the form of a combination of the national currencies participating in the credit-issuance; deutschemarks, francs, etc. Under the proposed reform, gold backing for the dollar would be achieved through U.S. participation in these joint-currency development credits.

4

The Creation of Credit

There are, generally speaking, two alternative methods for large-scale creation of added volumes of "fiat credit." One mechanism was adequately outlined by J. M. Keynes —through a centralized, private banking system. The better method, that of what used to be known as the American System, is through the issuance of governmental treasury, or national banking notes as new currency issue.

In fact, with the existing institutional framework, the generation of credit for world expansion needs will be a combination of the two methods.

It is the generation of fiat credit in the form of currency notes issued through national banking which is most poorly understood today. Clarifying that method provides the basis for subjecting the matter of private credit generation to analysis.

The usual, automatic response to the announcement that this reporter proposes to issue new U.S. Treasury currency notes as the means for credit expansion is a sharp outburst of horror! The auditor exclaims, "But, that's inflationary!"

This reaction ebbs, at least somewhat, as this reporter explains: The new notes are not to be issued against federal government operating deficits, but on capital account. The new currency notes are to be put into circulation through national banking channels, such as participation in loans

John Quincy Adams (President, 1824-1828) preserved and expanded the Second National Bank of the United States, and oversaw its most productive period in generating credit to build American economic strength. The scrapping of the bank by his successor, Andrew Jackson, resulted in a collapse of U.S. credit in the Panic of 1837.

issued for hard-commodity production and productive-capital loans through the local private bankers of ultimate borrowers.

Therefore, *the amount of fiat credit put into circulation through such channels is regulated by the following principal considerations.* It is limited by loan demand on account of tangible production's capacity, technological improvement, and operating capital requirements, and by the demand for such uses of credit among creditworthy borrowers. Each increment of new fiat credit issued through such channels supplements private banking capital also participating in the loan. Therefore, fiat credit is not put into circulation except against a matching increase in newly produced, tangible wealth providing security for this credit issuance. These are the immediate built-in regulators of the amount of such credit issued: the securing of the credit issued by the tangible wealth created through its use by creditworthy entrepreneurs which is the twofold, crucial consideration.

Therefore, *such forms of circulation of increased fiat credit could not be inflationary.* Directly the contrary, insofar as it occurs in a climate of promotion of scientific and technological progress, *such increase of credit energizes correlated rises in national productivity, and is therefore deflationary.*

That point outlined, we may proceed then to the next of the points subsumed under this topic.

Why, in any case, should fiat credit be allowed? Could we not, for example, simply increase the rate of savings to the point required to meet the need for investment and loan capital? The answer to the latter proposition is an unequivocal "No." There is no circumstance under which savings from current income could be augmented to fulfill adequately this function, *in a sustainable way.*

Current income is, by definition, the sum of current payments for both direct production costs and for administrative, services and other non-productive, "overhead" costs. Unless the economy is operating either at a loss or is simply stagnating, the sum of the "overhead" costs cannot be as large as the total gross operating profit of the society's tangible, useful output. Hence, there exists a margin of required credit in excess of current income, a margin which some British-influenced leftists hold up as proof of inherent "over production tendencies" in a capitalist economy.

It is desirable, in fact, that this margin of output in excess of current income paid be rather large. *This is the margin of net profit of the economy, the margin which determines the quantitative extent of possible expansion and technological expansion.* It is the realization of this margin of net operating profit as development of the economy, which determines, in the first degree, the ability of the economy to overcome entropic tendencies toward stagnation and decay, and, in the second degree, the rate of possible development.

Hence, a healthy economy requires a margin of newly introduced fiat-credit equivalent to this margin of excess of produced values over paid out current income.

Of course, nothing good is accomplished unless such added margins of credit are, in net effect, steered into the act of realization of capital improvements in productive potential. It is possible to generate much larger amounts of fiat credit, and yet, because that fiat credit is improperly invested or otherwise spent as current income, a counter-productive, inflationary result is produced.

The most efficient policy for solving both problems is to curtail all generation of fiat credit except through issues of currency notes on capital account by a national banking system, or similar discipline maintained for a centralized private banking system.

Governmental fiat credit should be issued, except under conditions of national emergencies such as wars, *only in the form of currency notes loaned on capital account*, either to economic ventures of governments (wealth-creating state investments), or through private banks as participation credit for medium- to long-term loan capital for hard-commodity production investment and production operating capital or export credit.

In the banking system more generally, the desired dirigism is effected by establishing a two-tier system of credit. High-performance borrowers of loan capital for production investment and production operating capital on medium- to long-term should enjoy a low rate of borrowing cost. Soft loans, including loans for secured assets in nonproductive ventures, should be made on condition of a discriminatory, higher rate of borrowing-cost, with undesirable degrees of "soft" perishable consumer purchases excluded altogether.

In addition, increases in state fiat credit on capital account means that reserve ratios for the private banking system should be generally higher than during recent decades. This is a feasible and desirable policy, provided that adequate government fiat credit is provided as participation credit.

Therefore, credit expansion is not in itself inflationary, and, furthermore, properly directed flows of government fiat credit in the form of currency notes circulated on capital account carries the relatively least risk of being diverted into channels of usage which are inflationary.

Which is to emphasize again that Professor Milton Friedman's conceptions of monetary processes are inherently incompetent.

5

The Economic Basis for Credit Expansion

We now begin our examination of the misguided economic objections to credit expansion. We begin by addressing a misguided, but unfortunately widespread assumption.

In this commonplace, naive argument against credit expansion, misinformed persons propose that a national economy's budget can be analyzed according to the same procedures a housewife might employ for budgeting her family's relatively fixed monthly income. In the course of the U.S. presidential nomination campaign, this reporter was astonished to discover how widespread toleration of that sort of delusion had become.

The crucial point is that the housewife's budget must be constructed on the basis of the assumption that the family's monthly income is relatively fixed. The state budget must be designed to facilitate a rapid growth in national income.

If the national budget (and related central banking matters) are subordinated to the principle of a relatively fixed national income, the result must be only more or less disastrous. At the very worst, such nominalist confusion over the meaning of the word "budget" in two different species of context, means promoting early economic collapse. At the least, such confusion over the meaning of terms unleashes an impulse of economic stagnation, among

Photo: U.S. Bureau of Reclamation

Broad-scale productive improvements in land, industrial capital stocks and resource recovery are the immediate purpose of large-scale credit expansion. California's water management infrastructure is the basis for the highest sustained agricultural productivity in the world. Parsons Engineering Co., has proposed a California-modeled "water grid" for all of North America.

policy influencers, promoting the preconditions for probability of a later economic collapse.

As summarized in the prefatory portion of this report, at any point in time, an actual economy is the net result of the strife between two opposing impulses. The one impulse is *developmental,* as we described that. The opposing impulse may be termed *devolutionary* or *entropic,* as we described that.

If we analyze a national economy competently, we treat the economy as if it were, in its entirety, analogous to a single agro-industrial firm. We analyze the accounts of this "firm" in terms of the rigorous distinctions for useful, tangible output, as opposed to overhead costs of administration, services, and so forth. This we do as this report specified in an earlier subsection.

All real national income is restricted, by definition, to useful, tangible output of agriculture and industry.

The various costs of administration, services, military expenditures, and sheer waste, such as unemployment, are the overhead expenses of the "firm," which are paid out of the gross operating profit earned, solely, by production of useful, tangible output.

If a net operating profit exists, after deducting overhead expenses plus debt service, from gross profit earned by production of tangible, useful wealth, then the "firm" is capable of surviving. However, its long-term survival depends upon an adequate rate of investment of the net operating profit in new purchases of technologically advanced, more capital-intensive productive capacity and output.

Only if that condition is satisfied can the developmental tendency be caused to predominate over the devolutionary impulse.

We admit, and also emphasize, that in the last analysis, the same principle can be proven to underlie the economy of a household. If the cultural mode of life of the household does not improve, the household will become either absolutely or relatively culturally-technologically obsolescent. However, *over the short-term*, this underlying, longer-term consideration is not empirically significant. Therefore, the housewife manages the household budget, quite properly, as if that underlying consideration did not exist. Her method is merely linear.

As we have outlined the additional point earlier in this report, the margin of credit required to circulate the portion of output corresponding to net operating profit cannot be squeezed entirely from the portion of the money supply cycled through payments for the inputs of production and overhead expenses of production. An additional margin of credit must be added to ordinary credit (savings), if the margin of product corresponding to net operating profit is to be reinvested.

This isolates the economic side of the policy matter on which our attention is focused here: *credit expansion.*

Once we acknowledge the fact that credit expansion is indispensable, the policy problem is narrowed by definition. At this point, we place ourselves in the position of a banker: *what assurance do we have that the credit expansion will stimulate a greater increase in pre-debt-service operating profit than is represented by the debt service incurred through credit expansion?*

Obviously, if credit expansion is deployed for increasing employment in gambling casinos, drug traffic, prostitution, social work occupations, nonproductive labor-intensive make-work by government agencies, and so forth, credit expansion becomes, axiomatically, purely inflationary. If credit expansion is applied to finance growth of state and private administrative bureaucracies, without a greater accompanying expansion in productive output, axiomatically the application is also intrinsically inflationary.

If the margin of investment necessary to maintain predominance of developmental over devolutionary impulses is not employed to increase technologically progressive, more capital intensive forms of production of useful, tangible output, the devolutionary impulse predominates. Worse: the result of such misallocations of credit expansion is to increase the ratio of cumulative debt to per capita real output for the national "firm" as a whole. The result achieved must be a rise of debt-service obligations relative to earned net operating income. This spiral will tend to continue past the point that aggregate debt-service obligations exceed net operating income. That latter is the normal cause for business cycles, and the determinant of the onset of successive monetary crises, and the onset, ultimately, of economic depressions.

From such general considerations, we are obliged to impose dirigist credit policies. We rightly insist that credit expansion must be channeled into technologically progressive, generally more capital-intensive modes of production of more productive output of useful tangible wealth. As a corollary of the same point, we conclude that, *in general, all business-cycle disorders, including inflationary spirals and economic depressions, are the direct consequence of a failure to maintain proper dirigist principles in national credit and taxation policies.*

Our commitment to a "hard-commodity-only" doctrine for capital application of credit-expansion funds is moderated by only one kind of consideration:

In classifying administration and services as "nonproductive," we indicated that certain aspects of administration and services, such as science, engineering, and teaching, were directly, causally positive, for increasing the negentropy of modes of production and potential productivity of the labor force. This benefit of such classes of services, and of the organizational functions of administration, *is not expressed as an economic output of the economy in its own terms.* Its real contribution is located entirely in the maintenance and improvement of *potential* national productivity. Actual national productivity itself is expressed exclusively in terms of useful, tangible output for that capital or household consumption which occurs in an economically regenerative mode.

As a society advances qualitatively in technology (productivity), its dependency upon certain administrative functions and productivity-enhancing services increases. The required increase in number of employed scientists and engineers per 10,000 industrial operatives employed is exemplary of this relationship.

If C plus V [$C+V$] represent the combined material and labor costs of production for a national economy; if d is chosen to symbolize combined overhead expenses, including services; if S represents the gross profit of production; then, (S-d), or S' may symbolize *net operating income*. Then, the ratio, $S'/(C+V)$, represents the social reflection for the potential rate of growth of the economy; and the value of the ratio, $d/(C+V)$, can be examined in terms of the requirement of a secular tendency for increase in the value of the ratio, $S'/(C+V)$ [15]

In general, it should be policy to hold the magnitude of d sufficiently low, that the rate of profit $[S'/C+V)]$ undergoes a net increase—without arbitrary reductions in real wages, or capital "asset-stripping."

In practice, this policy means that the priority for increase in the scale of services is limited to the following basic categories:

• Employment and training of increased ratios of scientists.

• Employment and training of increased labor-force ratios of engineering and related professionals.

• Employment and training of public school and higher educational institution teachers qualified to nurture scientific-technological potentials of students.

• Employment and training of public school, and higher-educational institution teachers qualified to promote mastery of the classical musical, painting, architecture, and literary heritage, as the notion of classical education is exemplified in conception and relevance by the 15th-century, Neoplatonist Golden Renaissance.

• Professional medical services for improvement of the longevity and maintenance of the physical and biological-mental substructure of individual human creative potential.

• Development of and employment of cadres of administrators trained and oriented as nation-builders, as leaders of organized effort to the ends of nation-building.

Certain other classes of services—fire protection, police services, military services—arc indispensable, of course.

In a well-ordered republic, citizens employed in the protective services, as exemplified by military services, give only part of their adult lifetimes to those occupations. Since military science and services center around logistics and related considerations of the most modern levels of technologies, the approach of Lazare Carnot, Scharnhorst, and the U.S. Military Academy's emulation of Carnot's program under Superintendent Thayer, exemplify the proper economic policy approach to protective services. This approach produces the relatively best quality of protective services, and also equips the citizen in such service to acquire the highest qualifications for outstanding performance in other occupations.

Since any modern republic continues to require a mass-based military reserve capability, constituted around professional military cadres, the economic approach to this aspect of national policy is to emphasize the logistical (science, engineering) leading element of modern military science and practice. The object of this is to make the costs of military functions a positive, educational expenditure respecting the development of the labor force and economy as a whole.

In summarizing this necessary interpolation on administration and services, we now say this.

It is possible to quantify the determination of permissible upper limits for the value of the ratio $d/(C+V)$, with respect to any corresponding value for the ratio $S'/(C+V)$. Such values for d should be exceeded only in respect to the fact that time is required to transmit the benefits of science and education into measurable results for the productivity of the economy as a whole. Proper policy begins with a determination of a quantifiable reference-value for the ratio $d/(C+V)$. Policy making allows that value to be exceeded only on the basis of extraordinary need for increase of protective services, or as a calculated investment in the future benefits of a presently increased outlay for science, engineering, education, medical services, and training of improved qualities of administrative cadres.

Now, we have focused the point under consideration more narrowly. We may shift the focus of our attention to the "ability" of productive investments to "carry" the costs of combined fiat credit and other loan and equity investment. This statement situates the economic basis for credit expansion in its most essential terms.

On what basis can we be assured that the net operating income generated by technologically progressive, more capital-intensive productive output will be able both to carry the debt service incurred, and also to provide a sufficient ratio of residual net operating income, after deducting debt-service costs to maintain the rate of growth of such investments? That is the kernel of the proposition confronting the prudent banker in this matter of credit expansion.

The simplest way to develop a rigorous response to that banker's proposition, is to begin with a brief statement of the methodological problem of reconstructing economic history to provide conclusive proof for the principles deserving the title of "economic science."

Thermodynamic Historiography

Although the "delphic" G. W. F. Hegel is not to be degraded to the same low class, intellectually, as Professor Milton Friedman, the two have a certain point of kinship, in their respective post hoc, ergo propter hoc approach to human history.[16]

Contrary to Hegel, there does not exist that sort of metaphysical "World Spirit" which automatically orders the succession of the principal forms of human society according to a principle of progress. Too frequently, a phase of progress in human development has been succeeded by monstrous disasters. A simple time series of historical forms of societies has therefore no intrinsic empirical authority for adducing a principle of society's development.

What we are obliged to do is to discover, first, criteria by which various kinds of societies can be ranked. By means of such criteria, we can then adduce from studies of the various empirical cases of progress and retrogression, so defined, what are in fact the principles which have governed efficiently development or devolution.

The required criteria for assessment of human societies can be nothing but criteria which gauge the increase or dimunition of the possibility for continued human existence. The simplest expression for that is the possibility of sustaining an existing or expanded population. This, in turn, is most usefully expressed by the notion of *relative population density*. To define the point more rigorously, we must measure *relative potential population density*.

Since the Club of Rome and allied institutions have not only broadly repopularized the absurd thesis of the British East India Company's propagandist, Thomas Malthus, but have terrorized credulous people with frightening images of "standing room only" upon our planet, it is necessary to put the latter evil fairy tale of the self-styled futurologists out of the way.

In the final analysis, the economic justification for an unending increase in the human population is this. Each human individual, unless biologically damaged in respect of the biological substrate of mentation, has the potential to be developed as what present conventions term a "genius." The more geniuses available for assimilation into a general division of labor in human creative discovery, the higher the rate of development of the quality of our species per capita.

So, the present period's real problem of population is not the numbers of individuals in existence, but the poor quality of development of most of those individuals.

Meanwhile, we are still a great distance in time from the point that the earth reaches a population density equivalent to that of present-day Belgium.

Insofar as we can extrapolate two centuries ahead, to the point that the earth's population might approximate the densities of today's Belgium, we must not overlook our species' stubborn laxity respecting the conquest of nearby solar space. We should have established, already, pioneering groups of exploratory teams on the Moon and even Mars, living there in artificial environments. We should have accomplished this already, had we managed our affairs competently over the course of this present century. We should be there, in the words of Sir Edmond Hillary, speaking of Mt. Everest, because nearby space is "there." We should be there because the tasks of exploration of our universe and its lawful ordering—to increase our dominion over nature—is an expression of our intrinsic purpose as human beings.

To some, the emergence of mass entry into space by humanity is variously inconceivable, or simply an unrealistic proposition. Yet, if we properly assess the fundamental breakthroughs in technology already imminent in advances at the frontiers of ultra-high energy flux density, and if we can conceptualize, with aid of that knowledge, what the potential rate of successive breakthroughs can be beyond that frontier, a very substantial human intervention into nearby space is an eminently realistic prospect for the coming century.

For that exploration, and associated subsequent colonization, over the coming two centuries and more, we shall require massive numbers of highly qualified persons.

A paleolithic man, squatting, breeding progeny mindlessly in a cave-home, implies intolerable over-population of the earth with the increase of population to a few millions. If we, unlike such a wretched cave-dweller, get about our proper business, and look upward to the next category of tasks before us, the prospect of future "overpopulation" evaporates.

In any case, we emphasize again, the present problem of population is the relatively poor *quality* of individuals, not the *quantity* of persons. This point is underscored with great and painful force for us, the moment we turn discussion to the problems of economic development among emerging nations of the southern hemisphere.

Putting neo-Malthusian and equivalent means for terrifying of credulous children to one side, we return now to the matter of *potential population density.*

By examining the thermodynamic implications of the modes of agricultural and other production characteristic of various cultures, we begin to construct the kind of economic historiography we require.

We find that the potential relative population density associated with a culture located in this or that portion of our planet in various epochs, is to be correlated with the per capita rate of throughput of energy. A certain mode of production is associated with increases, over inferior cultures, in the useful energy per capita associated with that mode of production. This involves not only increasing the energy input per capita. The ability to concentrate available energy in such a fashion that what is termed the "free energy" of the throughput application increases in ratio to the total energy throughput of the process within which production is situated.

So, we have the three associated conceptions of energy before us: 1) "raw" energy-throughput per capita, 2) energy flux density, and 3) the tendency for the rate of free energy to correlate with energy flux density. The combined increase, per capita, of the total energy, energy flux density, and free-energy ratio is, in turn, the correlative of what might be termed the "reducing power" of that cultural mode.

That increase in "reducing power" per capita is the correlative of potential rates of relative population densities.

We noted earlier that this cultural mode defines certain aspects of nature, as altered by mankind, as an associated array of "relatively finite natural resources." In general, were a culture to persist in an unchanged mode, it could not maintain even a constant level of population. The depletion of the domain of natural resources defined by a fixed culture increases the marginal cost of exploitation of resources. This, in turn, reduces the ratio of the "free energy" to the total energy throughput; that in turn, reduces the potential population density. This leads to a contraction of the culture's population, as well as the basis for sustaining that culture, and leads, in turn, to a devolution of the mental and physical quality of individual life.

"Cultural relativism" is dangerous nonsense. The definition of relatively superior and relatively inferior cultures is not only rigorous, but is a conception of the utmost importance for maintaining the survival of civilization generally.

In consequence of the double cost of both offsetting devolutionary impulses (entropy) and securing net development, the rate of effective energy throughput per capita for cultures increases more rapidly than the increases in potential population density resulting from development.

If we rank cultures in a reconstructed time series, according to the criteria outlined above, we discover that not only does the rate of required energy flux density increase in terms of an exponential function, but that the rate of increase also rises in terms of an exponential function. Today, the energy flux densities uniquely available through successive development of fission energy and fusion technology energy production must be made the characteristic mode of energy production, or else civilization can not survive (at best) long into the next century.

These advances in mode of production are, in the last analysis, effected through the equivalent of what we term today fundamental scientific progress. It is the increase of man's mastery of the lawful ordering of the universe, the perfection of the development of the mental creative potentialities of producers according to such scientific progress, which enables mankind to effect advances in the thermodynamics of human existence. It is the effective organization of the productive application of energies of greater free-energy ratios and higher energy flux densities which is the substrate of the possibility for continued human existence.

The Market Fallacy

The foregoing establishes the basis for most efficiently examining a commonplace, fallacious argument against the perspective of a general expansion of world trade in capital goods.

It is argued that the world market is presently constricted, saturated, and contracting. It is proposed, in consequence of such noted trends, that the market potential needed to sustain an investment boom in world trade does not exist.

This fallacious argument against credit expansion has two distinguishable philosophical origins. Viewed in the narrowest, most immediate terms, this focus on "existing market demand" is a *monetarist* fallacy. Yet, the same fallacy is also, alternatively premised on a somewhat different school of thinking: the "materialist" school associated most prominently with the succession of Adam Smith, David Ricardo, and Karl Marx.

Today's currency is merely paper. It can be reorganized, as President de Gaulle and Jacques Rueff did with remarkable success. Terms of lending can be regulated in many ways, with variously disastrous (Volcker), or beneficial effects. Credit can be created in relatively vast amounts, by a mere political decision, and the credit created can be applied either prudently to promote growth, or insanely, to promote hyperinflation. Changes in taxation policies can alter the flows of investible income drastically, and can increase or decrease substantially the rate of savings.

In matters pertaining to currency, credit, and monetary systems, there is no "invisible hand." There are merely misinformed persons, so blinded by ignorance of illusions that they cannot see the very mortal and substantial human hands, which seem to do anything to paper values they choose—up to the point that more powerful, equally mortal hands determine otherwise.

The question is not how much market demand exists, but how much new market demand we shall create, and under what rules, for its application.

The other, non-monetarist premise for the kind of fallacious argument reported is premised on assumptions which deny, either overtly or at least implicitly, the actual source of the wealth of society.

For reasons we have stated above, and for analogous reasons given by Hamilton, the sole source of true wealth of society is improvements in the productive powers of labor. The margin of society's economic surplus dependent upon the continual increase in the productive powers of labor, is the portion of total output which determines the scale and profitability of investment markets in the succeeding epoch.

The commodity speculator believes that "profit" is essentially a matter of buying low and selling high, more or less on the basis of a pre-existing market demand. The commodity speculator's philosophical cousin, the rentier-financier, believes that profit is essentially the interchangeability of rent and debt-service income as a tax upon pre-existing production levels. Neither understands real profit; neither understands the most basic principles of venture capitalism.

Venture capitalists invest not merely in existing markets. In the final analysis, they invest in the production of *new* masses of profits at *higher rates of profitability* than generally available earlier. This profit for which they invest is created by *the increased margin and amount of net operating income created through constantly improved productive powers of labor.*

This increased productivity of labor has two, interdependent mediations. Basic advances in scientific knowledge are mediated into production by way of relevant forms of improved education of the labor force's households' members, and by what Hamilton classifies as "artificial labor." The latter is the increasing capital intensity of investment in technologically progressive modes of production, through which the ratio of high energy flux density production-energy to human muscle-labor is constantly increased.

Our "market" is ultimately a member of the urban labor force in an emerging nation, who has the equivalent or approximation of a European level of technological culture, and who is variously presently unemployed, or employed in a relatively labor-intensive mode of production. With proper application of capital, we can increase that latter person's productive output by approximately an order of magnitude. Those define the prime, immediate investment opportunities.

Another portion of our market is undeveloped agriculture. Given proper political leadership of even illiterate or semiliterate farmers in these nations, infusions of modern agricultural technology in the form of irrigation, better stocks, proper fertilization, and prices providing investment incentives, will increase the per hectare and per man-year output by up to an order of magnitude or greater over spans averaging a decade.

More generally, by assigning one or two generations of development to bring the most-distressed strata of the populations up to the standards of modern labor-force potentials, we are nurturing a greatly expanded investment market for the future.

What we must do is to establish financing mechanisms which use the high rates of gain, from premium grades of short-term investment opportunities, to carry the medium-to long-term financing of development of future investment potentials. A high rate of profit can be developed for premium investments, even after taxing part of the whole profit produced, to subsidize financing of medium-to-long-term development of future investment potentials.

It is convenient to view prominent Third World economies, or groups of less developed nations, as if they were single agro-industrial firms. We develop the "firms," each as a whole, by concentrating on rapid promotion of potentially high-gain agricultural, manufacturing, mining, transportation, and energy production projects. This generates an increased operating income which can be set aside in three categorical subsections. One section carries the financial loan costs of investment on the high-gain projects. Another section is used as profit margins for expanded investments (equity costs). A third section is contributed to payment of debt-service charges on account of medium- to long-term development of the future potentials of relatively marginal portions of the populations.

Putting to one side, for the moment, the crucial political leadership aspects of nation-building endeavors, the critical financial management problem to be overcome is the present need for a gold-pegged reserve currency (or, currency of account, such as a gold-pegged ECU), through which medium- to long-term loans may be denominated in low rates.

The related policy problem is that of building a global development policy around a set of well-defined leading priorities.

Priorities of Policy Formulation

The clearest of these priorities is the adoption of a nuclear energy program.

The best estimate available so far is that meeting the energy requirements of the world for the year 2000, under conditions of development at sound rates, requires between 5,000 and 7,000 new gigawatts of electrical energy production. Most of this must be supplied by combinations of fission, fission-fusion hybrid, and fusion reactors.

This is imperative for two reasons. First, only the successive advances in energy flux densities proferred by progress from fission to fusion technologies can place the world in the position to meet critical requirements including large-scale desalination, and overcoming of emerging raw-materials bottlenecks during the early decades of the next century. Second, for reasons of combined supply and cost of fossil fuels, and the potentially catastrophic environmental effects of either enlarged fossil fuel or "soft energy technologies" packages, fission and fusion sources are the only adequate, cost-stable, and environmentally acceptable large-scale source of the majority of essential electrical and process-heat energy over the coming decades.

The important possible economic objection to constructing new generating capacities with an investment of between $5 and 7 trillion 1979 U.S. dollars-equivalent over two decades is the apparent lack of production resources adequate for such an undertaking. That technical objection reflects a bureaucrat's habituated lack of imagination. Specifically, the proposed undertaking means the global equivalent of an economic war mobilization, using such precedents of reference as the U.S. wartime Manhattan Project and the more recent achievements of NASA.

This very problem proves to be a major part of the solution to our policy-making problem. The extension of the bills of materials and process sheets for providing upstream supply for constructing the equivalent of 5,000 fission energy power plants of 1,000 megawatts each means such things as an investment revolution in the world's metals industries.

In general, the only workable approach to nuclear energy installation is the nuplex approach. New industrial centers, including their energy plants and other industries, must be developed as packages—unitized combinations assembled on requirement, as one developmental construction package—like assembling collections of interchangeable parts. The creation of energy-producing capacity, and the mating of that capacity with the industries using the electrical power and process-heat, is clearly the only acceptable approach for most cases.

This packaging requires a war-mobilization-like expansion of ocean freight and riparian traffic.

The second leg of development is the priority to be placed on agricultural development. This will have an impact comparable to the scale of nuclear development already cited.

The spread of famine and epidemic would be sufficient reason to emphasize agricultural development. Over the medium to long term, another consideration emerges as predominant.

The introduction of high-technology agricultural development to Europe's southern tier, and to the emerging nations' region generally, will have two leading, combined long-term economic effects.

First, the measure of economic development of a national economy, and hence its potential productivity and profitability is the reduction of the portion of the labor force required for producing a high level of nutrition. OECD nations must reach about 4 percent by 2000 A.D. India must reach 25 percent by about that time or slightly later. Mexico must reach about 10 percent—and so forth and so on.

Some degree of specialization will help to reach this goal.

The United States is losing vegetable production excessively, its beef and dairy production are threatened with significant contraction, while the independent farmers, the backbone of U.S. agricultural productivity, are being savaged by current Carter administration programs. The United States can and must increase its acreage, especially in grains, beef, dairy, fruits, and vegetables.

There are analogous potentials in the great agro-industrial region of South America's Rio de la Plata sector. In the longer term, the Sahel must emerge as the grain belt of Africa.

While technological progress in agriculture contributes crucially to national growth and productivity, modern agriculture is the largest single consumer of industrial products. The development of agriculture is therefore one the greatest levers for sustaining long-term expansion of domestic markets.

The commitment to such priorities will engender an unprecedented rate of turnover of invested productive capital in capital-goods-exporting nations. This will occur on a scale more significant in degree than we have recently noted in the export-oriented industries of Japan and the Federal Republic of Germany. This means rapid rises in the general rate of productivity, and associated expansion of rates of investments in new capital-goods technologies.

This is not the location in which to continue elaborating the effort to be made. What we have said so far adequately illustrates the point. It is advances in the productive powers of employed labor, which is the only ultimate source of real wealth, and the only ultimate market for investment.

Instead of destroying economies to accommodate to the relics of an old, decayed monetary system, develop a new monetary system which fosters investment in technological progress.

With one word of caution, one can say that Karl Marx did not comprehend this. In his contribution to *The German Ideology*, and the concluding fragmentary section of *Capital* III, on "freedom and necessity," he states the proper principle. In his hysterical refusal to acknowledge the error of his corrupted attack on Friedrich List, Marx never understood the principles of an actual industrial capitalist economy, and therefore relegated the adduced possibilities of actual industrial capitalist development only to a socialist economy. Most specifically, he, like all those "materialist" political economists he exemplifies, refused to comprehend that all capitalist productive investment—as capitalist investment—ultimately depends upon investment in technological advancement of the productive powers of labor, and not the buying-cheap and selling-high misconception of the regulating role of the existing commodity markets.

Notes

15. The symbology used here is not Ricardo's or Marx's *in content*. It is defined in the initial published reports outlining the LaRouche-Riemann Model.

See Uwe Parpart and Steven Bardwell, "Economic Development," *Fusion*, July 1979.

16. Sec treatment of Milton Friedman by Mrs. Joan Robinson in her *Economic Heresies: Some Old-Fashioned Questions in Economic Theory* (New York: Basic Books, 1971). As far as she goes in attacking Friedman, Mrs. Robinson's ridiculing of his post hoc ergo propter hoc methodology is quite sound. For a fuller treatment of Friedman, see Lyndon H. LaRouche, Jr., and David Goldman, *The Ugly Truth About Milton Friedman* (New York: New Benjamin Franklin House, 1980).

6

How Policy Should Be Formulated

We emphasized, earlier in this report, that the world could not be in today's manifoldly perilous mess if wrong policies had not been adopted and tolerated. We noted that the private elite institutions, both national and multinational, which, predominantly, have shaped the policies of the dominant OECD nations, have either served as vehicles for conduiting neo-Malthusian and related doctrines, or have lacked the qualifications to provide effective alternatives to neo-Malthusian influences.

In the United States, this reporter's candidacy for the 1980 Democratic presidential nomination led to the establishment of the National Democratic Policy Committee, an institution which will become an exemplary new policy-formulating private institution of the variety urgently needed in numerous allied nations.[17] We now summarize the special features and implications of this Policy Committee, and of required private circles, to perform similar kinds of essential functions in other nations.

This concluding portion of our present report has the included function of situating the principal monetary-economic policy issues of the report within the appropriate, policy-formulating context.

Photo: Carlos de Hoyos/NSIPS

Lyndon LaRouche and Helga Zepp-LaRouche (at right) in policy discussion of countermeasures against international narcotics traffic in late 1979, during LaRouche's campaign for the Democratic presidential nomination.

So far in this report, we have emphasized the "objective," scientific aspect of policy. We have outlined issues of policy as they might be adopted, abstractly, as the special knowledge of a single individual, or of a relatively isolated elite group of scientific specialists.

The instant we focus on the implications of the term "policy," we require that correct policies be viewed not merely as the privileged knowledge of an isolated few specialists. *To develop correct policies as an organic part of the actual policy-shaping processes of society, we must define and establish the appropriate forms of social processes for "organically" generating policies and making knowledge of the correctness of those policies integral to the judgment of large portions of the "rank-and-file" citizenry.*

We must define the characteristic features and tasks of private institutions capable of developing correct policies. These institutions must be so interlinked with political parties, banking, industry, agriculture, and trade unions, among others, that the special private policy-formulating institutions are in effect an agency of the organized strata of citizenry to which the special institutions are interlinked.

In some respects, the kind of new institutions required do differ entirely in appearance from existing varieties of national and multinational policy-deliberating bodies. A required sort of institution is not efficiently interlinked unless it includes bankers, trade union leaders, farmers' representatives, industrial executives, as well as scientists. Formally, notable existing private institutions appear to fulfill or approximate those kinds of "organic" qualifications.

Furthermore, many of the existing private elite entities have the qualifications to perform a useful part in giving new directions to the policy-formulating process.

To understand the difference between the proposed new generation of policy-formulating entities, such as the National Democratic Policy Committee, and the "think tanks" generally dominating the situation up to this point, we must contrast the general character of the existing entities with those with which the NDPC initiators find closest kinship from the past.

Models From the Past

In the history of the United States, the most prominent model of reference is Benjamin Franklin's "junto" network, which organized the establishment of the United States as a Federal constitutional republic based on the American System of political-economic policy. In France, there was the network of organizations of *les politiques*, centered around such institutions as the Oratorian order, maintained around the included task-orientation of developing bridges and highways, and continued by the École Polytechnique under the leadership of Gaspard Monge and Lazare Carnot. In Germany, there were the Lafayette-allied republicans, typified by the publisher von Cotta and Friedrich List. The latter developed the American System of industrial power for Germany through strategic focus on railways, powered river-traffic, forced development of metals and chemical industries. In Japan, there is the example of the conspirators behind the Meiji Restoration, who initiated the industrial revolution of Japan according to the adopted American System of Hamilton, the Careys, and Friedrich List.

The characteristic common to these cases is this.

These bodies were dedicated to *a certain conception of statecraft*. This was predominantly a dedication of *nation-building around directed policies spanning a horizon of generations to come.* They shared consciously, or by significant influence and in approximation, the conception of statecraft prominently associated with Gottfried Wilhelm Leibniz.

Franklin's policies, for example, conspicuously emulated those of Leibniz.

Although most among these circles were dedicated nationalists, these were chiefly circles which maintained close connections to similar circles of other nations, and, in most cases, situated their nation-building policies in the context of a global policy like that of the "grand design" of France's Henri IV, and G. W. Leibniz.

For example, beginning 1766, at the time leading American circles dedicated themselves to an inevitable break with Great Britain, Franklin used his connections as a leading scientist to integrate the American republican effort with the Oratorian-centered circles of French republicans, and with the Oratorian-linked European-wide networks of followers of Leibniz. It was the resources of this transatlantic conspiracy, centered around Franklin, which ensured the victory of the American Revolution.

At the close of the American Revolution, a section of Franklin's transatlantic conspiracy was consolidated in the form of the Cincinnatus Society, an organization of both U.S. and European military officers who had served in the American Revolution. During the period following the 1815 Treaty of Vienna, the Marquis de Lafayette assumed international leadership of the Cincinnatus-based political-intelligence networks, and actually headed the U.S. intelligence organization working against London and the Holy Alliance forces in Europe. It was this network which provided a crucial margin of assistance to the industrial development of Germany.

The *republicanos* of Mexico overlap, in origins and initial development, the same circles which produced Carnot and Lafayette in France, and the allied "French" networks of mid-18th-century Spain and "New Spain." This connection was the historical basis for the alliance of Abraham Lincoln and his immediate circles to the Mexican *republicano* circles associated with Benito Juarez. The important German connection into Mexico, featuring Humboldt, overlapped the U.S.A.-France-Germany linkage via Lafayette's networks. That history is the organic basis for the strong affinities between the *republicano* nation-builders of present-day Mexico and the political-philosophical heirs of the founding fathers in the United States today.

It is the complementary conceptions of nation-building and global "grand design" which exemplify the special, Leibnizian notion of statecraft, a conception which has been lacking in influential, elite policy-formulating transatlantic entities of the recent period.

It is the establishment of private policy-formulating entities which revive such practices of statecraft required and proposed for this period. It is from that standpoint that the proposed monetary and economic policies can be viewed as practicable, as well as objectively imperative.

Modern Statecraft Historically Defined

We term this Leibnizian notion of statecraft "modern statecraft," a term which properly emphasizes the decisive earlier role of this conception in bringing into being the modern, sovereign, industrialized nation-state.

To understand the basic principles of modern statecraft, to proceed to master the methods and procedures of policy-shaping this statecraft represents, we must begin with an outline of the history of the emergence of this conception within the context of Apostolic Christianity's shaping of Western civilization.

If this reporter now repeats, essentially, what he and some among his immediate associates have published in other locations, such repetition is unavoidable. These are not only the conceptions upon which this reporter's outlook and method are ultimately premised entirely. They are correct, indispensable conceptions, which have been driven out of the knowledge of most otherwise literate and educated people at all levels of policy-making influence today. Therefore, until that lack of knowledge is adequately remedied, this "lost knowledge" must be identified anew in each location until it is directly an essential premise of the points of action being recommended.

In locating our notion of statecraft within the self-development of Western civilization, we are obliged to emphasize that our civilization is a product of Apostolic Christianity. (Ostensibly civilized persons, who deny that fact thereby attach to themselves the term otherwise applied to persons who profess themselves to be offspring of unnamed fathers.)

This definition just stated does not imply ignorance of the indebtedness of Apostolic Christianity's culture to Rabbi Philo Judaeus, the personal ally of St. Peter. It does not imply ignorance of our great indebtedness to the Arab Renaissance led by the Baghdad caliphate, or the debt to the culture of India through such giant intellects of the Arab Renaissance as the genius with the tell-tale name of ibn Sina. It does not imply ignorance of the adoption by Apostolic Christianity, as shown most emphatically by Rabbi Philo's influence, and most authoritatively, by the writings of St. John and St. Paul, of Christianity's professedly Neoplatonic concurrence with the methodology of Plato. Nor does it ignore Apostolic Christianity's hostile contempt for the degradation and tradition of Roman culture and the immoral system of Roman law modeled on Aristotle's "Nicomachean Ethics." St. John and St. Augustine are adequate examples of authorities on that latter point.

The line of development of Western civilization under Neoplatonic Apostolic Christianity's influence is first consolidated under the leadership of Charlemagne and his counselor Alcuin. This inaugurated an effort to establish a *republic of Christendom* in "grand design" alliance with the Baghdad caliphate—an ecumenical alliance in the sense of ecumenicism later rigorously defined by the great 15th-century canon Cardinal Nicholas of Cusa.

The efforts of Charlemagne and his successors in this direction were constantly harassed, and occasionally ruined by forces centered around the families of the old Roman imperial oligarchy. These adversaries of Christian civilization, adversaries usually working under the cloak of a counterfeited Christianity, used two correlated methods, repeatedly. These methods were employed in the effort to resurrect the oligarchical design which the Roman Empire had emulated from the fourth-century B.C. "Persian model" design for a "Western Division of the Persian Empire." Those two commonly used methods were first the use of delphic cults to organize barbarian intrusions of looting and conquest into the civilized regions of Europe, and, secondly, the use of pagan and pseudo-Christian gnostic-modeled cults to foment Jacobin-like, Khomeini-like antiscience, antirationalism, antitechnology destabilizations from among the most superstitious, brutalized strata of peasants and vagabonds within civilized regions.

The Vikings were deployed under such a Hesiodic cult against France. They were used later in a coordinated assault from Scandinavia and Normandy against England. The leading families of Rome and Venice coordinated with Genghis Khan, and promoted the westward movement of the Mongol forces.

Later, during the 15th century, when an ally of the Golden Renaissance forces, the Paleologue, was bringing his forces of Byzantium into cooperation with the forces centered around Cosimo de Medici in Italy, the same gnostic families of Rome, Genoa, and Venice organized and equipped Muhammad the Conqueror's forces for the assault on Constantinople. It was the Genoese mercenaries in Constantinople that opened the gates of the city to the Turkish military, and the Italian families who provided Muhammed with artillery and the technology for their use.

The defeat and murder of the last heir of the Hohenstaufen and the forced abdication of Hohenstaufen ally Alfonso the Wise—during the last half of the 1260s, set into motion a hideous devolution of European civilization. The inquisition against England's Roger Bacon is exemplary of the gnostic cultists' deployment of Khomeiniac-mullah-like inquisitors against science, rationality, and technological progress, during the last half of the 13th century.

The policy of "controlled disintegration" and "IMF conditionalities" which the victors over the Hohenstaufen imposed, with aid of bankers such as the notorious Bardi and Peruzzi, caused a process of depopulation of Europe, such that half the parishes of Europe vanished between the fall of the Hohenstaufen and the middle of the following century. Fraudulent accounts of this depopulation attempt to attribute it entirely to the bubonic pandemic of the 14th century. The pandemic is estimated, at most, to have reduced the existing population of its time by one-third. The pandemic was merely the last phase of a larger reduction of population, caused chiefly by interconnected effects of famines and epidemics.

The population of France did not reach mid-13th century levels again until the latter part of the 18th century.

Contracting the productive basis while spiraling refinanced indebtedness of both major and minor potentates became a self-aggravating spiral. Indebted landowners reduced the numbers of serfs by increasing the hours and days of labor on the landowner's portion: to increase means for paying debt service. This resulted in an "asset stripping" of accumulated improvements in agriculture. The commerce and production of the urban centers withered through this decay of the agricultural sector.

The displaced and unemployed increased the ranks of hungry, desperate vagabonds, and so also the numbers of thieves, and of bands of locust-like roving banditries. Potentates sought financial relief by conquering and looting other potentates. Standing military forces were therefore augmented by both looters and defenders. The combination of a prevailing "guns-not-butter" policy in practice, with devastating looting increased the vagabondage, the famine, and the proliferation of epidemic disease.

The Horsemen of the Apocalypse were unleashed upon Europe.

It was into this spiral of devolution and depopulation that the Spoor Mongols brought the leading contribution of Old China's culture, bubonic plague. Just as the Mongols had depopulated the decaying, Asharism-devastated Islamic world, so the weakened populations of ravaged Europe offered a pathway of reduced human immunities for spread of this product of pre-Maoist culture.

It was in the setting of this "new dark age" that a circle of Augustinian republicans, typified by Dante Alighieri, developed the policies leading toward the 15th-century emergence of the modern, sovereign, industrial nation-state. It is Dante's work, situated within the larger scope of Apostolic Christianity's development of Western civilization, which is chosen, most efficiently, as the point of reference for tracing the development of modern statecraft.

The fatal flaw in the earlier efforts to develop a republic of Christendom was the correlated obligation to adopt the Latin language as the language of administration, science, and culture, as well as of religious institutions. This aggravated the condition of the common speech of the people, as a collection of degenerating, brutish, illiterate local dialects.

This perpetuated a circumstance in which the population generally lacked the power of communicating important conceptions, or even rational thought. *A people which cannot communicate important, rational conceptions, lacks the power to think rationally.* It is a population susceptible to manipulation by that plague of mullah-like friars, which spread like a pestilence across Europe in former times. It was this aspect of the condition of society, the intellectual and moral depravity of a brutish, superstitious proletariat, which had been demonstrated to be, repeatedly, the fatal flaw inherent in the otherwise noble design for a republic of Christendom.

The analysis of this mental problem, at various levels of the populations, is rigorously examined in its essential features and dynamics in Dante's Commedia. From that standpoint, most of the people of Europe, together with much of both gentry and priesthood belonged to the brutish, existentialist immorality of the "Inferno" canticle—and most among them proximate to the pit.

The solution to this cancer of brutish, immoral superstition within European society must include the transformation of debased local dialects into groups of common, literate languages, languages transformed to impart to the user the power, as Shelley puts it, to communicate "profound and impassioned conceptions respecting man and nature."

This task is the principal focus of modern European statecraft from that time onwards—at least, until the approach of this present century. Exemplary is the case of Miguel Cervantes' great, polyphonic, Platonic dialogue of a prose-drama, Don Quixote. The subject is the successive transformation of outlook in the process of attempting to qualify a typical poor, gluttonous, unstable peasant, Sancho Panza, to become capable of governing an "island." The issue, the task, was to elevate the brutalized, superstition-ridden common people to a level of cultural, intellectual, moral development, at which such persons would become capable of competent self-government.

The sovereign nation-state, based on the subordination of heteronomic local dialects into a literate, cultured common language, must be the new form of society.

This new policy, consolidated as a policy during the 15th-century Golden Renaissance, is not only a program for developing particular, sovereign nation-states. It is also a "grand design." It is the dedication of the forces shaping the development of such nation-states to making those republican principles effectively a world order of humanity.

We may observe, with much emphasis, that this program was sufficiently implemented to bring the peoples of some nations to a condition of popular literacy and culture in which they proved themselves qualified for self-government. They have usually failed to govern themselves well; but, even in their repeated failures, there was clear evidence of great progress from their 14th-century brutalized ancestors.

It should be clear to us, in lapsed-time, integrated overview of the manifest results of policies of leading nations over the course of this century—since the fall from power of France's Gabriel Hanotaux and Russia's Count Sergei Witte—that our general situation has swung from the generally upward course into the early 20th century, downhill. The rate of descent is now accelerating, especially since 1967. Growing proportions of the industrialized nations' populations are reverting, notably under the spreading disease of the "rock-drug counterculture," to a parody of the irrationalist, superstition-ridden rabbles of the 14th century.

Meanwhile, as we examine our leading universities, our leading policy-formulating think tanks, our leading political parties, the leading cadres of industry, finance and other callings, we appear to have lost effective knowledge of those essential principles of modern statecraft we have violated to repeatedly hideous effects over the course of this present century.

The Inner Dynamic of Statecraft

Merely educating the illiterate and their wretched little local dialects, to use a common, literate, rationalist language, does not fulfill, in and of itself, the requirements of modern statecraft. There is an indispensable "inner dynamic" which must govern the process of education.

The quality which distinguishes the human being from mere cattle is the ability of the human species to become conscious of a lawful ordering of the universe, and to dedicate itself to govern human practice by a commitment to ever more perfect discovery and mastery of that lawful ordering. Cattle's behavior is by nature a zero-technological-growth behavior. When mankind does not exercise its divine qualities, its power to master and be governed by the lawful ordering of the universe, its scientific creative intelligence, man is degraded morally as well as intellectually to a brutish condition.

Although it has been the essential distinction of the republicans over millenia, that they are city-builders, and although scientific-technological progress is indispensable to continued existence of our species, it is not individual material gain in and of itself which is the motivation of the city-builder's policy. The essential motivation is that portrayed in St. Augustine's *City of God*. Scientific progress is a moral principle of civilization, because without practical emphasis on that quality of development and exercise of human creative potentials which scientific progress mediates, man slips, in and through practice, into a zero-technological-growth condition of cattle-likeness, of relative bestiality.

For just such reasons, the proposal to adopt a space-exploration perspective for mankind now is not dependent upon predetermination of any precise practical benefit from that endeavor. The proposal must be adopted, because the development of man as man requires that mankind always move to a new, greater scientific undertaking than mankind has previously accomplished.

Now, we turn to the crux of this matter. This is the point which determines, variously, proper scientific method, the proper principles of poetry, drama, music, and literate speech. It was what is most frequently named the principle of *hypothesis*. It is that principle which properly governs the directed development of the language, thought, and statecraft of a people.

We apologize for the fact that the following paragraphs must, once again, impose description of a technical sort on the reader's eyes. It is the reporter's policy that every key premise of a proposal must be reported to those to whom the proposal is presented. The reader must know of the fact of the existence of the premises, whether or not the reader is pre-qualified to judge the technical, internal features of that premise or not.

We have identified the fact that we are able to rank, rigorously, conclusively, relatively inferior and relatively superior forms of culture. By methods which correlate directly with such conclusive empirical demonstrations, we can rank the ordering of lesser and higher degrees of scientific knowledge. It is the general notions and associated methods of an adducible cultural level of scientific practice, which reflect the *potential* "reducing-power" of that society. So, one level of scientific development can be rigorously, conclusively ranked with respect to another.

The interconnection goes deeper.

The practical expression of scientific progress is increases in the various thermodynamical facets of productive progress: energy throughput, energy flux density, free-energy ratios. The process subsuming successive advances in the thermohydrodynamics of the modes of production we have termed "negentropy."

The *ontological* significance of negentropy *is not that of a construct*, but of *the primary form of material ontological existence in the universe*. That is, a transfinite function which is in the most immediate correspondence to *what is not ontologically ephemeral*.

The negentropy expressed as the relative transfinite for successive progress in modes of production is the equivalent for the notion of *higher hypothesis* in the dialogues of Plato. This notion is central to all of the principal work of Bernhard Riemann, as well as Karl

Weierstrass, Georg Cantor, and the Leibnizian predecessors to Riemann's notion of hypothesis, as that is summarized in the habilitation dissertation referred to earlier here.

It is also, as we shall now report the proof, the governing principle of the use of the method of the Platonic dialogue by the Golden Renaissance Neoplatonists, including Cardinal Nicholas of Cusa. This was employed by them and their heirs to order the development and internal-developmental features of what came to be known as classical literature, classical music, and classical painting and architecture.

Ordinarily, *hypothesis* signifies the synthesis of an experimental insight (experimental design) according to rigorous principles of necessary reason, in terms of the *existing* level of development of scientific knowledge in general. No experimental hypothesis is *ordinarily* acceptable unless its form is coherent with the ordering of the universe consistent with existing levels of advancement of scientific knowledge as a whole.

That notion of ordinary hypothesis requires us to employ a somewhat different term, *higher hypothesis*, to identify the principle being addressed here.

The existing state of advancement of scientific knowledge as such, is but one of the two principal categories of rational knowledge available to us at any time. The other, rigorously defined category of rational knowledge, is *the evidence corresponding to the successive advances in levels of scientific advancement leading up to the present.* By making each of these successive levels our primary data of reference, we pose the problem experimentally: *What principles of hypothesis order this succession?*[18]

This rigorous approach to this latter, classical problem of epistemology yields an hypothesis—*a higher hypothesis* —which is correlative to the notion of negentropy given in this report. Moreover, this approach demonstrates, as was also demonstrated in Plato's dialogues, what is underlying and permanent ontologically, in respect to the lawful ordering of the universe.

Every particular level of scientific knowledge is ephemeral. Hence, all definitions of things and relations according to that specific level of knowledge are ephemeral definitions, and relate specifically to ephemeral conceptions of reality. What is not ephemeral, is that which determines a succession in levels of knowledge, and in a manner consistent with empirically-demonstrable negentropy. What is not merely ephemeral, is that transfinite which persists in the reflected form of the ordering of successive advances in the levels of scientific knowledge.

The naive person, the miseducated person, views the progress of science as a process of correction of previous "errors," describing knowledge as thus convergent upon an error-free point of axiomatic termination of all further, valid new discovery. Yet, by correlating advances in levels of scientific knowledge with advances in the negentropy among properly ranked societies, the application of the term "error" to any of the levels of scientific knowledge in such series is shown to be itself axiomatically the worst sort of error in fact.

Error in human practice, or scientific knowledge in particular, is that specific kind of conceit which moves us backward, toward the sort of cattle-like moral bestiality presently demanded by the radical neo-Malthusian Utopians. Any transformations of knowledge which move mankind forward, as shown by the metric of negentropy, can not be an *error*.

The erroneous notion of *error*, which we have just ridiculed for its absurdity, reveals to us a misguided mind which has confused reality with getting good marks on school-room examination papers.

We have already far too much of that instruction suited for mere parrots, in which pupils are drilled in prescribed "right answers," are drilled to the purpose of being thus enabled to make passing grade selections for each multiple-choice question in an examination, or to exert themselves to the slightly higher planes, of regurgitating the memorized "right word" to fill in a blank of an examination question. The pupil becomes a trained "information-regurgitator," who is passed or failed respecting his "human mental development" by an idiot of a mark-sensing computer.

It is admittedly cheaper to provide such schooling and grading procedures for such featherless parrots, than to develop the powers of a human being to be able to think rigorously and creatively. It is the ability of the student to discover a truth which the teacher did not know in advance, but which competent teachers are obliged to recognize as a proper discovery, which is the object of *human* culture, and of the education of *human* beings.

"Classical culture," meaning the classical heritage of the Golden Renaissance's method for developing culture, is focusing literacy and the shaping of the uses of literate forms of revolutionized common language, on the principle of the higher hypothesis.

In scientific education according to this principle, we educate 10,000 qualified, terminal degree-holders in advanced science, by a method designed to ensure that at least a dozen or so among them will demonstrate the capacity to effect valid fundamental breakthroughs, thus to open the way to higher levels of scientific knowledge than presently exist. We will train 10,000 such by methods designed to produce the equivalent Gaspard Monges or Bernhard Riemanns, and will realistically content ourselves that this effort has produced only a dozen or so such. At least, most among the remainder of the 10,000 will be qualified to assimilate and develop further what the relative handful among them achieve.

The "unit" of scientific-empirical reality is not the well-defined, isolable thing; it is the smallest interval of action in a process of negentropic development of the whole process. It is that shift from reductionist to scientific world-outlooks, a shift communicated by the method of the Platonic dialogue, which is the empirical locus of the "inner dynamic" of statecraft.

The principal reader's difficulty in connection with the foregoing point is the result of the now-habituated misconception that *Geisteswissenschaft* and *Naturwissenschaft* are unrelated inquiries. This misconception can be made credible only to the extent that physical science is degraded in conception to mechanics. At the level of Riemannian physical geometry, the notions underlying the conception of the most generalized "Riemann surface" are identical with the classical Neoplatonic argument for *consubstantiality*.

In fact, the principles of the Platonic dialogue, as exhibited in the Bach-Mozart- Beethoven-Brahms principles of composition according to principles of well-tempered polyphony, as exhibited in the dramas and poetry of Shakespeare and Schiller, in the painting of the school of Raphael, are identical with the method of the Platonic dialogue employed by Johannes Kepler to establish modern physics.

In ancient India, as well as in Plato's dialogues, principles of literary composition are used to communicate principles of geometry and physics in a rigorous, fully competent manner. Giordano Bruno, among others, revived the techniques of using poetry to prove principles of physics.

The primary object of statecraft is to adduce the divine within the human individual, and to nourish the individual's self-conscious perfection of that mental-creative potential, to the purpose of producing a culture fit for a society of the geniuses the common citizen of the future will be. We work to achieve the *City of God*, the New Jerusalem.

A society in the process of development toward that ultimate objective is a true republic, a true member nation of the "grand design."

Elitism in a Democratic Republic

It is the private citizens of a nation who comprehend, and who are self-governed by that vision as their adopted purpose, who are properly the philosopher-kings, the Neoplatonic elite of a nation. They are not ivory-tower speculators, but practical leaders of various aspects of life —statesmen, scientists, great entrepreneurs. They represent a selection of the best of all of the crafts of the city-builder, the nation-builder.

As private citizens, they are like a Roman citizen praised by Niccolo Machiavelli. This Roman republican, called from his home and private labor, to lead his nation's military forces, completed that duty with distinction, and then, his assignment completed, returned to his home and private labors. That is the quality of the true republican elites.

Without such republican elites performing their function of leadership, no nation of modern civilization can avoid hideous catastrophes.

Is this an "anti-democratic" sort of "elitism?" Those who performed judicial murder on Socrates would insist that it is "anti-democratic."

In Dante's *Commedia*, there are three canticles, the "Inferno," "Purgatory," and "Paradise." Today, the "Inferno" is represented by the existentialists, the irrational "environmentalists," the dionysian cultism of the "rock-drug counterculture," and the like. Herein lies the principal, direct internal threat to all existing democratic republics. The condition of "Paradise" is the condition of but a few properly leaders of elites. Most of the ordinary, good, moral citizens of nations belong to the category of "Purgatory."

These Purgatorians, our "average," moral citizens, have a characteristic flaw of underdevelopment. They are almost continually dominated in outlook by fixation on matters such as personal career, pensions, and other objects of "earthly paradise," as Dante outlines the problem. They may wish that the consequences of their living and acting will become in effect something worthwhile which lives after them. Unfortunately, excepting unusual periods of self-mobilization, as under conditions of perceived grave crisis, these "average" citizens are unable to think rationally in terms of the policy interests of the society as a whole.

These ordinary, moral citizens adopt a substitute for rational comprehension of national policy matters. That substitute is a collection of slogan-like rules-of-thumb. To the extent this collection of slogan-like rules has a pragmatic correspondence in moral-practical effect to what national policy interest would require, we speak of the "good conscience" and "morality" of the average such citizen.

For related reasons, the mechanisms for political party direction of such underdeveloped citizens center around the use of political slogans, which act as a moral-principle-like substitute for rational analysis.

This practice is, to a certain degree unavoidable, as long as citizens cannot muster themselves to rise above that underdeveloped state of conscience. In the short term, parliamentary policy making, and the related election process, is degraded to a competition among contending good, wicked, useless, and merely foolish sorts of political campaign slogans. Over the longer term, under competent practices of leadership, the level of rationality of the average citizen is raised by successive degrees, bringing such citizens closer and closer to the level of competence, to think about policy matters directly and rationally.

It is a correlative of this, that citizens usually do not vote for a policy. Rather, most citizens vote for one party, one candidate, *as a way of voting against* another candidate or policy.

The citizen does not wish to govern. The citizen, in general, has the same kind of reluctance shown by Sancho Panza when exposed to the opportunity to be a governor. The citizen does not wish to forego the pursuit of personal "earthly paradise" goals of mortal, individualized security and related gratifications; the citizen is unwilling to make the personal intellectual and related dedications which, to that citizen, appear to be a "sacrifice" of personal and family goals. *The citizen is usually democratic only negatively*, not in a positive sense. The citizen does not desire to govern; he wishes to only retain the power to oust governments and policies which offend his sense of what he wishes to tolerate.

For related reasons, today's mass-based political parties are instruments of parliamentary government, but usually lack the moral and intellectual qualifications to define competently important policies.

This is the difficulty which confronts that elite which is dedicated to the democratic-republican objectives of Dante Alighieri, Miguel Cervantes, and others of that same outlook. *How can we maintain and develop the forms of democratic-republican institutions, while efficiently providing those institutions with the competent policy perspective and policies which neither the general citizenry nor major political parties are presently capable of discovering?*

If we do not succeed in this, then the existence of democratic-republican institutions will continue to be the relatively short-lived, more agreeable resting-places for mankind, between the dictatorial regimes—"emergency decree" governments, dictatorships, and so forth—which appear each time a nation falls into a crisis which democratic political institutions prove themselves organically incompetent to overcome.

True, the coup d'etats which are more or less seasonal events in Latin American and other emerging nations, occur less frequently in industrialized nations with a higher average level of popular culture. The thresholds for breakdown of democratic-republican institutions in nations which are culturally more advanced is much higher than for less developed sections of the human family. Only hideous disorder, such as that imposed upon Weimar Germany by Versailles and the London short-term-credit committee, produces dictatorship in nations with as high a level of culture as Germany.

This latter aspect of the picture encourages us, since it demonstrates clearly that the progress of European civilization up to the beginning of this present century, had established a level of culture not so far beneath that at which truly durable forms of democratic-republican institutions are attainable.

Therefore, to restate the proposition: *How can we compensate for the policy-formulating incompetence of mass parties and the general electorate, without resorting to a method which impairs democratic-republican institutions?*

The uniquely acceptable answer to this challenge is that *the solution lies in the domain of influence, rather than fiat-rule.*

In large degree, the Anglo-American elite circles which have directed postwar policies of governments already rely on methods of influence, aided by effective control over major news media, entertainment media, and over many other major institutions of intellectual life. They also own politicians, political parties, and other key directive institutions top-down, and also governmental bureaucracy. The notion of influencing policy of nations by initiatives of private elite circles is scarcely novel in this period. That, in fact, is the way in which most so-called democratic nations are presently governed from behind the scenes.

The difference to be noted lies in the characteristics of the kinds of policy-influencing ideas to be generated, and the internal characteristics of the method by which these ideas are to be generated and interrelated. It is in those respects that modern statecraft urgently requires private institutions of a different quality than has predominated over the postwar period to the present time.

The problem, as we see it clearly enough in the behavior of most leading governments, is that even the best political leaders simply lack a clear perception of the quality of policies the present situation requires. They lack such alternative policy outlooks, because they and other leading institutions lack adequately institutionalized sources of policy formulation offering such alternatives.

If a statesman today says to himself or to his immediate, trusted circle, "This policy isn't going to work, but it's the best, to my knowledge, among the choices available," where can he turn to find a better alternative? In practice, today's quality of politician lacks those extraordinary potencies required to seek alternatives from any but what he or she regards as a limited range of accredited sources of policy-making counsel. If these accredited sources do not provide the needed alternative, as far as the statesman is concerned, such alternatives simply do not exist. He does not search further.

The same is true for the community of bankers, industrialists, trade unionists and so forth. The same is true for the citizenry generally. Today, the statement heard more and more frequently from more and more of our average moral citizens is, in effect: "Obviously, the present situation is intolerable. The political parties are incompetent, and present policies will probably simply make the situation worse. But, what other choice do we have?"

If alternatives were *institutionalized as accredited ideas*, the very conditions of what is increasingly perceived as a worsening crisis would define most of the leading institutions and citizenry as disposed to consider adopting such alternative policy conceptions.

It is in that indicated fashion that the conscience of the ordinary citizen may be periodically reformed, brought into line with new realities, that the citizenry will replace old, become-counterproductive slogans, with new sets of slogans appropriate to the generation or so of work before the nation at that juncture.

Thus, suitable private assemblies of elite circles, circles guided by the principles of modern statecraft, must be assembled to provide a new influence of *institutionalized ideas*. These must be provided simultaneously to

statesmen, political parties, business, trade unions, farmers
and the citizen generally. These circles must, at least
collectively, comprehend the way in which the
characteristic features of ideas put into circulation shape the
development of national culture and institutions organically
over periods of a generation or longer.

The Form of the Elite Circle

The historical key to the proper form of policy
formulating circles is the view of statecraft associated with
Leibniz and the École Polytechnique under Monge and
Carnot. Policies of education, military science, physics,
political economy, musical composition, and so forth
constitute an indivisible subject matter. We may promote a
division of labor, such that a specialist may emphasize
excellence in one or two aspects of the whole subject
matter. Just as political economy does not function except
as a mediation of scientific progress, it is only by
reassembling the elements of the division of labor into a
single, integrated whole, that policy can be formulated
competently.

To have a strategic policy, a science policy, an energy
policy, a credit policy, a tax policy, an exports policy, an
educational policy, and so forth organized in such a fashion
that each of these aspects of the matter is treated
independently of the others is commonplace practice. It is
also a monstrous folly.

The proper constitution of a policy-formulating group is
the assembly of leading figures of finance, industry,

agriculture, and labor around a group of leading scientists and political economists. The last should be of the sort adduced from this report.

The task is to determine what present and prospective basic science can accomplish to solve the problems defined in the indicated method of political-economic analysis. The other participants—apart from the scientists and political economists—represent institutions through which the possibilities of scientific progress are to be realized. It is in the interplay between the leaders of production and the scientists that a policy competently spanning two generations into the future can be rigorously elaborated.

From the vantage point of such a policy-formulating outlook in general, subsumed, short-term policy-formulating problems can be effectively treated.

The time and the funds must be found to bring together frequently key figures representing such a combination. By establishing such additional sources of policy-formulating in key nations, and by establishing consultation among such circles in various nations, a new, urgently needed dimension of transatlantic policy-formulating is to be developed.

This work conduited into existing channels of radiation of policy-formulating conceptions, will make practicable that which is needed so desperately, as a new set of policies, for this period.

Notes

17. The National Democratic Policy Committee is a Multi-Candidate Political Action Committee, certified August 30, 1980 by the Federal Election Commission under the Federal Election Campaign Act. The Committee's Advisory Board is chaired by Lyndon H. LaRouche, Jr., and includes Julan Jack, former Manhattan Borough President; David Samuelson, Travis County (Texas) Commissioner; Dr. Morris Levitt, Executive Director, Fusion Energy Foundation; Dr. Robert Moon, Professor Emeritus in Physics, University of Chicago; and Art Wilson, farmer, Cholame, California.

18. This is identical with the generalization of hypothesis by Riemann's famous habilitation dissertation--cited several times during this report. It is also the principle underlying Georg Cantor's elaboration of the notion of transfinites. In contradistinction to the bowdlerized version of "Riemannian geometry" usually offered by textbooks, as in the mistaken Einstein-Weyl program, Riemannian physical geometry is as we reflect it here. The notion of the higher hypothesis is central to both the notion of a generalized Riemann surface, and to understanding the significance of higher-order Abelian functions in Riemannian differential functions.

Made in the USA
Middletown, DE
29 May 2020